THE ENGAGEMENT BANKING REVOLUTION

How to architect banking around the customer
and thrive in the platform era

Written by Change Makers

The Engagement Banking Revolution

Editors: Patrick Aalbers, Le Raine Hendrik, Aleksandra Miljus, Mike Perkowski, Al Perlman, and Matthew Todd.

Copy Editor: Andy Fordham

Design and composition: Gabriella Guigue and Ben Ledger

Produced with grateful thanks to all the employees and partners of Backbase, who continue to power the Engagement Banking revolution every day.

Publisher: Backbase B.V.

Backbase B.V., Jacob Bontiusplaats 9, 1018 LL, Amsterdam, The Netherlands.

Phone number: +31 20 4658888

First published: 2022

Limit of Liability / Disclaimer

The Engagement Banking Revolution, contains summary information about banking and financial services. The content is a reflection of the input provided in interviews with the mentioned Change Makers. The content is current as of its initial publication date February 2022. Although the book may be revised and updated at some time in the future, the publishers and authors do not have a duty to update the information contained in the book, and will not be liable for any failure to update such information. Neither the publishers and authors nor those interviewed make any representation as to the completeness or accuracy of any information contained in the book.

The book is written as a general guide only. It should not be relied upon as a substitute for specific professional advice. Professional advice should always be sought before taking action based on the information provided. Every effort has been made to ensure that the information in this book is correct at the time of publication. The views expressed in this book are those of the authors or interpretations of those interviewed. The publishers and authors do not accept responsibility for any errors or omissions contained herein. It is your responsibility to verify any information contained in the book before relying upon it.

Backbase is proud to support the FT Financial Literacy and Inclusion Campaign with the proceeds of *The Engagement Banking Revolution* book sales.

The FT Financial Literacy and Inclusion Campaign works with partners to deliver clear, compelling content on basic financial subjects to the people who need it most all around the world.

This educational campaign will help decode the financial world, and give people straight answers on crucial issues—from credit card interest and student loans, to taxes and how to start a business.

To learn more or make a donation, please visit ftflic.com.

Table of contents

Welcome to the revolution

Jouk Pleiter, Chief Executive Officer, Backbase

This book is a call to action. A playbook. A guide. Perhaps you might even think of it as a manifesto. We sincerely hope you will use it to lead changes vital to your customers and necessary for our industry.

All of us, collectively, have an opportunity to enhance the lives of our customers and help them to better manage their money; to deliver them newfound freedom to engage with their finances in ways that weren't possible even a few years ago.

What is happening in the banking industry is, as this preface's title suggests, nothing short of revolutionary. The ways in which people have banked and managed their finances for decades are changing right before our eyes.

Data is literally at our fingertips. Rich data. Data that didn't exist a few years ago. Data we can access using devices that fit in the palms of our hands. Data we can use to make decisions and take actions in seconds, from the convenience of our homes, without ever talking to another human. Real-time, contextual, actionable information, that comes with insights and intelligence that can change our lives for the better.

For our customers, it's all just a click away. For us banking leaders, it's all just a platform away.

What I'm describing is the proverbial tip of an iceberg of opportunities to enhance people's lives and create an ecosystem to open new revenue streams for banks. The possibilities are endless. You're likely well aware of what is taking place in banking and how quickly things are changing. You don't need an entire book to explain what's happening. And that is not our intent.

Our intent is to help you discover what you can do about it; how you can be active participants in the revolution rather than passive observers. To achieve that goal, we've brought together 13 experts from across and beyond the banking industry. In this book they share their wisdom, experience, expertise, and real-world ideas and concepts that you can put into practice. Immediately, if necessary.

Over the course of the book, our authors explore what's taking place on the ground in the banking industry. They examine the impact being made by the FinTechs and Big Techs, and the threat posed to existing business models. They explain what Engagement Banking is all about; why it's revolutionary, and why there's an urgent need for banks to embrace new business models and viewpoints.

They also look at the underlying technological innovations that have made the revolution possible. They explain how your organization can maximize new technologies like cloud computing, open standards, and—most profoundly—the shift to engagement platform models to affect change and empower your customers in previously unconsidered ways. Platforms are the most profound shift because, ultimately, it's the single platform model that makes Engagement Banking both possible and necessary. What we've seen in platform economics across myriad industries in this century is now revolutionizing banking. Think

Amazon in retail; Netflix in home entertainment; Apple and Spotify in music; Uber in transportation. The list goes on. If you're a leader at an incumbent bank, you'll want to leverage the power of an Engagement Banking platform to fuel your innovation, rather than be restricted by existing systems of record and the binary decision to build or buy.

Another important purpose of this book is to give you peace of mind by showing that Engagement Banking is not only possible; it's already happening all over the world.

Yes, it's true that digital transformation is daunting. Yes, it impacts business models, cultures, processes, and relationships with customers. And yes, it will impact your fundamental view of what your organization is and how it engages with the world.

But this type of transformation is also right within your grasp and power. Now. Hundreds of banks, no different than yours, are successfully navigating the transformation to Engagement Banking and reaping the rewards. You'll find many examples in the pages of this book.

A lot of thought goes into creating a book such as this, and I want to thank everyone who has contributed, especially the authors, who have taken the time to share their ideas. For me, it's been a fantastic learning experience. Ultimately, when I think about what it is that we want to accomplish, I usually come back to the idea that we want this book to inspire. At Backbase, we believe in Engagement Banking with all of our hearts. We live it every day. We experience it on the ground.

We've watched banks transform from bricks and mortar to digital. We've seen their customers transform from frustrated to engaged. We've listened to individuals all over the world thanking their banks for welcoming change, and for listening, and for delivering the kinds of experiences they had never imagined would come from their banks.

We know what it's like to create a bank people love. And we know how rewarding it is for leaders who take an active part in that process. We know it can be done and we know you can do it. We want you to experience the excitement and commitment of doing something special; doing something in your work that has long-term meaning and sustainable value.

We want you to embrace Engagement Banking. And not just because it's the right thing to do for your business or your career, but because it's the right thing to do, period. You have an opportunity to make people's lives better. We want this book to inspire you to seize it.

Welcome to the Engagement Banking revolution. We may have started without you, but there's still much work to be done.

Let's do it.

Jouk Pleiter

The revolution
has begun

Chapter 1

Why do people love platform businesses?

Tim Rutten, Senior Vice President of Strategy, Backbase

I'm a music lover, audiophile, and "hobbyist" musician. I listen to all kinds of music, and especially love discovering bands or musicians I may not have heard before. I also like to share music that interests me with my friends and family.

Over the past few years, the platform application Spotify has been a revelation. It gives me everything I need and desire to pursue my passion. I can listen on any digital device, whenever I want, wherever I want—even when traveling. I can explore different types of music, and share it easily. In fact, Spotify even recommends music it thinks I'd like based on my listening habits and preferences. And, pardon the pun, its recommendations are often "spot" on.

Spotify is simple to use, transparent, and a welcome addition to my life. It enhances my enjoyment of—and experiences with—music in ways I could never have predicted or imagined. It's hard to even think about going back in time and picturing life before Spotify. I am thrilled that Spotify is available to me; that it is simple to use; and that it helps me in my daily life in ways that are friction-free, seamless, and convenient. I love to use it.

Is it possible to love **a bank** in the same way?

It is.

I've witnessed it first-hand. I have seen people fall **head over heels** for their banks... **because of their banks' digital banking apps.** In fact, I've seen users so in love with their banks—and their banks' apps—that they've needed to post publicly about them.

Users in Bahrain:

> *"This app changed my life. Easy and fast. I manage everything from the app. The account interest makes me money while I sleep."*
> - User on Google Play, February 4, 2021

> *"Incredible user experience! To think this comes from a few months old bank that not only shock the island but completely redefined banking standards."*
> - User on Google Play, February 4, 2021

> *"Great user experience, very easy to pay bills and excellent interface for other services."*
> - User on Apple, January 25, 2021

Users in Canada:

> *"I love this app because it makes it so efficient to quickly check on my banking needs and to quickly send e-transfers to family and friends in need!"*
> - User on Google Play, March 5, 2021

> *"Now I can see the whole picture of my banking info in a nutshell. It's so much easier to read and understand."*
> - User on Google Play, March 14, 2021

> *"Extremely easy to use. Now that I have started using it in the era of COVID-19, I may never go back to the branch for regular banking needs."*
> - User on Apple, April 7, 2020

Users in India:

> *"Online banking experience made easy and simple, with the added advantage of executing important banking transactions from the convenience of your hand-held device."*
>
> - User on Google Play, February 14, 2021

> *"In simple words: banking at fingertips. It's simple to use and covers all the transaction options that, as a customer, I need to carry out. Kudos to the team."*
>
> - User on Google Play, March 12, 2021

> *"One of the best hassle-free banking apps in India."*
>
> - User on Apple, July 29, 2020

People all over the world are falling in love with their banks and the modern digital-first banking applications and experiences they deliver. Customers are being engaged in ways they could never have predicted or imagined. And it's saving them time, saving them money, and reducing their stress—and they're appreciating the convenience.

In the last decade, we've experienced end-to-end disruption in customer experience and expectations. Music has been revolutionized by Spotify; home entertainment has been revolutionized by Netflix; retail has been revolutionized by Amazon; local transportation has been revolutionized by Uber. Now it's banking's turn.

It's the Engagement Banking revolution.

And it's happening just as rapidly as the revolutions in those other industries. Once people fall in love with a new way of doing things, they never want things to go back to the way they were.

There are two options for those of us in the banking business:

1. We can go about our business as usual and sit on the sidelines and watch as the revolution happens all around us, taking bites out of our legacy revenue streams until all we have left are crumbs.
2. We can join the revolution and go about building businesses people love.

One of these options is more exciting, engaging, satisfying, and lucrative than the other. I assume, because you are reading this book, you are interested in learning more about the Engagement Banking revolution and exploring what it takes to build a business people love. Hopefully, by the end of the book you will be inspired, committed, and prepared to begin or continue your journey.

Let's get started.

The common elements

The types of businesses people have fallen in love with so far in the 21st century share common elements in their make-ups. They are:

- Predominantly digital-first and digital-native—and in some cases, digital-only.
- Powered by and driven by data, including rich data analytics and insights, artificial intelligence, and machine learning.
- Inherently secure, agile, resilient, intuitive, simple, and trustworthy.
- Omnichannel—delivering a consistent, seamless, friction-free experience across mobile, web, and face-to-face platforms.
- Customer-focused to the 'nth degree.
- Able to deliver a 10x improvement in customer experience, simplicity, and value proposition.

Perhaps the most important common element is the delivery mechanism all these businesses share:

The digital businesses that people **love** today **are all built using the platform model.**

The platform model represents a fundamental paradigm shift across all industries and businesses. Companies that adopt a platform model develop a huge initial advantage over competitors. In a very short time, they can achieve that 10x improvement in customer experience and engagement.

But that's just the start.

Because the platform model simplifies the delivery of new services, and accumulates massive amounts of information and insight about customers, it allows users to continuously grow their competitive advantage over time. Platforms are like living, breathing, organisms—evolving with and adapting to customer needs.

Now is the time for banking institutions and financial companies to move into the platform era.

Big Techs and FinTechs have already had successes in taking away pieces of the financial services business. But it's not yet too late for any incumbent.

Banks still have tremendous value in customer loyalty across a wide range of services. They have years of data on all types of customers. They deal with customers on their finances, thereby forging trust and building relationships in one of the most intimate, private, and important aspects of people's personal and business lives.

These are the foundations upon which to build your bank's digital future. The foundations to lay to foster engagement with your customers, avoid having your business disrupted, and perhaps create a little difficulty-causing disruption for your competitors. It is doable, and it is doable for any incumbent bank, including yours—no matter where on its digital journey it might be today.

There is one other very important point to keep in mind.

Although it may seem daunting to shift to a platform model, it doesn't have to be overwhelming. You don't have to reinvent the wheel; you don't have to build everything in house; you don't have to hire hundreds of people; and you don't have to walk away from your existing technology investments.

With a purpose-built platform model, you can achieve visible results very quickly, delivering 10x improvements in key areas of customer engagement in a matter of months.

The journey

The journey to being a bank people love starts with a fundamental question:

"What are the jobs to be done?"

You don't need me to tell you what needs to be done—but you do need to go through this exercise with your teams and ask the question twice. First, ask the question from your customers' perspective: what do **they** need to do?

Answers might include: check balances and accounts; pay bills; manage investments; make myriad financial decisions based on real-world data; make payments; transfer money between accounts.

Now, how do your customers need to do those things?

Perhaps from their computers; on mobile devices; in person; at any time;

in any location.

When they do those things, how do they need their experiences to be?

Perhaps: intuitive; simple; friction-free; glitch-free and fast; instilling trust in their security and privacy.

Many of your customers also need their bank to help them be smarter and better informed about their financial decisions and opportunities.

So, that's all about the customer's perspective.

Now let's look at your bank's perspective: what do **you** need to do? From back-office functions, depending where you are on your digital transformation journey, your responses could include: eliminate data silos; shift certain applications to the cloud; create engaging new mobile services; modernize website; automate specific tasks; modernize business processes and business models.

When thinking about jobs to be done, I often ask people in banking to look for guidance in the kinds of applications they are excited about in their daily lives.

Perhaps they like to travel and use Airbnb. Or they like the convenience, simplicity, and reliability of Uber. Or maybe they're a Spotify fan, like I am. Those are all platform services that solve specific customer problems and eliminate friction.

Then I ask them to look at their own digital banking solutions.

- How proud are you of the digital services your bank offers, and would you love to use them yourself?
- Are there applications you are excited about and if so, why?
- Can you imagine your customers being excited about your digital offerings?

Too often, that excitement is missing. That needs to change. It's time banks thought like platform companies, and it's time to apply platform principles and ideas to banking.

As a bank, you already have the "most trusted" brand. It's highly unlikely your customers would prefer to bank with Google or Apple, because they haven't established the same degree of trust. But if the Big Techs or FinTechs offer a 10x improvement in engagement and you don't... all bets are off.

An Engagement Banking platform

So far, in discussing businesses that people love, I've focused on the consumer space. In that space, many of the companies that adopted the platform model were first to market, such as Uber and Airbnb. Others already had digital platforms that allowed them to expand their offerings—companies like Apple, Microsoft, Google, and Alibaba.

In retail, Amazon did it all: it created a revolutionary business model **and** built its own platform. It did it so successfully, it made it **almost** impossible for other retailers to compete.

Almost, but not completely. Amazon's success paved the way for another company to build a third-party platform for retailers. It is being used all over the world to power other businesses that people love, enabling them to successfully compete against the formidable Amazon platform.

That platform company is Shopify.

Shopify has emerged as the most trusted e-commerce platform in the world, used by more than 1.7 million businesses (and counting). As a consumer, you may be using the Shopify platform every day without even realizing; it's a business-to-business platform rather than a consumer platform.

Shopify is used by businesses to set up and manage their e-commerce operations from soup to nuts. It takes care of all the jobs that need taking care of; hundreds if not thousands of them. It configures websites, coordinates payments, and configures tax brackets. It handles customer-facing and back-office integrations, orchestrating entire value chains for customers and centralizing everything in one place.

Shopify does things its customers could never have conceived of doing. Even if they had conceived of them, many wouldn't have had time or resources to execute the ideas by themselves. What Shopify offers is an incredible solution. And yes: customers love it.

The same model is available in the banking industry. Most banks don't have the time, talent, or resources to build their own digital engagement platform. Nor do they have the desire to transform from a financial company to a technology company. Does yours?

The good news is, with a purpose-built, third-party platform, a bank can move into the digital realm very quickly. Within months, your bank could be competing as a platform player.

Our company, Backbase, aims to be the Shopify of the banking industry. We have the leading platform to enable banks to adopt a platform model and successfully join the Engagement Banking revolution. I'm not here to give you a sales pitch. But I do want to make it clear that **everything your bank needs to transform into a bank people love is achievable**—even if you're yet to take the first steps of your digital journey.

Banks people love

Most people don't love their incumbent banks.

Sorry to be blunt, but it's the truth. Too many banks are mired in traditional business models forged in the brick-and-mortar era and constrained by legacy IT infrastructures. The Engagement Banking revolution hasn't arrived in every bank. But it will. And soon.

Of the many banks where it **has** arrived, it's those that have shifted to a platform model that are reaping the benefits and rewards of engaged and satisfied customers.

And **why** do customers love those banks? Because:

- They get a simple, intuitive, and friction-free experience.
- Their data is in one place, consistent across every channel with a single dashboard.
- Insights are data-driven and personalized for each customer.
- There's fast decision-making with instant or near-instant results.
- There's no need to constantly provide their bank with the same information for different services.
- Their banking is mobile, secure, and always available from any device.

Once your bank can achieve those things, your customers will love you for it—and reward you with more business; and with referrals to their friends and family, and with positive comments and reviews on social media. Your bank will be the recipient of extreme customer loyalty and retention.

As I mentioned earlier, I've seen this transformation many times:

Techcombank, Vietnam

Techcombank is one of the largest banks in Vietnam and recognized as a pioneer in focusing on customers and their evolving needs. The bank's vision statement is *"Change banking, change lives."* To fulfill that vision,

Techcombank uses a platform model that allows it to build upon its own in-house design capabilities with a modular, scalable architecture that integrates quickly with various technologies.

The market for financial services in Vietnam is growing rapidly. So is the competition. To win in the market, they needed the best customer insights and the best way to engage with the customer. They also needed a platform model that could deliver the speed and flexibility they needed.

Techcombank is investing in three core areas: data, digital, and talent. The platform model enables them to operate as a hub whereby they can leverage their 360° view to help customers orchestrate their daily financial lives simply, seamlessly, and from any device or location. To measure the impact of this digital transformation, the bank is targeting improvements in Net Promoter Scores, real revenue growth, and the total number of interactions with each customer.

> *"For a bank right now, it's about full service and getting the digital engagement and personalization right. We need to talk to each and every customer as an individual, not a number, not a segment. We are here to help you achieve your life objectives, your business objectives."* [1]
> - Pranav Seth, Chief Digital Officer, Techcombank

Citizens Bank, United States

Citizens Bank is the third largest retail bank in the United States. For several years, the bank has been implementing a next-generation technology strategy based on five pillars: hiring high-caliber engineering talent; moving to an agile operating model; adopting APIs and modern microservices-based cloud native architecture; simplifying the IT landscape by taking a cloud-first approach; and developing core resilience. They wanted to start on a journey which allowed them to create a true test-and-learn culture, one which allowed them to look at every experience across the bank, and remove all the friction points.

By moving to a platform model, Citizens Bank has been able to build faster, add newer functionality at lower cost, and provide more test-and-learn opportunities. For example, Citizens built a new branch and ATM locator in five days—versus a process that would have taken at least six-to-ten weeks. Development has been remarkably faster than the bank has ever seen before.

The key to differentiating Citizens Bank in the digital world is in their responsiveness to the needs of customers.

> *"Where you win with the customer is the experience wrapper. That's how you begin to differentiate yourself and make sure your brand meets the needs of today's customer. Customers want to know that your content is driven by their own experiences. Our clients are changing, so we have to change along with them."* [2]
> - Lamont Young, Executive Vice President and Head of Digital for Citizens Bank.

Feeling the love

If you strive to build a business people love, you'll find the passion becomes contagious. Your customers will become engaged in new ways, asking for new services and features to make their lives better.

If you have a platform model that is flexible, digital, and adaptive, you'll usually be able to accommodate them—and **quickly**. It will become a virtuous circle leading to even greater customer engagement and therefore better results for your bank.

That contagious passion will often extend to your workforce—certainly to the people on your digital teams, and often to everyone who works at your bank. People, and especially younger people, don't want to work for organizations stuck in the past and unable to meet the needs of their customers. All employees would rather hear accolades than complaints, and deal with happy rather than frustrated customers.

In fact, your employees want engagement just as much as your customers do. Taking part in the Engagement Banking revolution will open you up to a broader employee base, positioning your bank to be a more innovative, exciting, and engaging place to work. If your customers love you, there's a better than even chance your employees will love you as well.

So, what's next?

How do you transform from what you are now to what you need to be? How do you embrace digital transformation in a way that may disrupt your business models, without disrupting your ongoing operations? Most importantly, how do you take the steps necessary to make yours a bank people love? How do you Spotify or Shopify your bank?

You have the time. You have access to the right tools and technologies. You have access to partners that can help you achieve best practices. And now, with this book, you have a rationale, a guide, and a roadmap. There's nothing stopping you.

Love may be just around the corner.

1. "Modernizing Techcombank for a digital transformation", Backbase.com
    (video case study), https://www.backbase.com/best-bank-in-vietnam-techcombank/
2. "Customers are in control", Backbase.com (video case study),
    https://www.backbase.com/citizens-case-study-connect-2019/

Chapter 2

Platform economics: how to increase banking revenue and delight customers

Interview with Sangeet Paul Choudary, Author; Founder, Platformation Labs

Banking industry executives talk enthusiastically and often about creating greater customer loyalty—in order to build and operate banks both consumer and commercial clients will love to do business with.

But the actions and policies of their banks often belie that goal, resulting in more fragmented use of their banks' products and services—and wider distribution of client banking dollars among both traditional and new, tech-savvy competitors.

Loyalty, and all the benefits that go with it for banks, cannot be achieved without true engagement. It's true engagement which makes repeated, efficient and profitable transactions possible. Through true engagement, banks can more easily and affordably offer new products and services to existing customers. It also helps bring new clients into the mix through sophisticated analytics to personalize offers and creates a customer experience that screams, **this is a bank you want to do business with.**

A lack of customer loyalty is hardly a new problem—especially in consumer banking. In 2016, 47% of U.S. consumers said they would consider Target or Walmart as an alternative to their traditional bank.[1] In 2019, 75% of consumers between the ages of 18 and 24 said they would consider banking with an established technology company.[2] It is undeniable that many banks have been on their heels fighting an entirely new set of competitors who play by different rules—and come with different strengths—than traditional banks.

Increasingly, forward-thinking banks are learning that leveraging a platform model is critical to winning user engagement in a connected world. That instead of staffing their branches with in-house experts selling everything from life insurance to wealth management advisory services, they can leverage platform strategy. With it, they can build a portfolio of composable services from affiliated, trusted third parties that connect to the bank and its customers through its platform.

An **ecosystem of partnerships,** enabled by **a powerful, open digital platform,** is a **better way to improve financial outcomes.**

Platform strategy is a core concept in banks creating more engagement in the face of rapid changes of all types—technology, buyer behavior, regulations, security, and risk mitigation, competition, and more. Such changes are causing the underlying structure of the banking industry to experience massive shifts. The balance of power is transferring from large, vertically integrated banks, to nimble, specialized upstarts that have used platform strategy to transform their value proposition quickly, less expensively, and more efficiently.

Defining the platform and its role in Engagement Banking

Now we've set the stage for the transformation from vertically integrated, siloed banking structures to a platform model, let's take a step back and define some core terminology.

At the heart of this chapter—and of this entire book, of course—is "the platform". I define "the platform" as a digital business model which enables innovation and manages interactions and coordination across an external ecosystem of producers and consumers. Platforms are built on open infrastructures, breaking down technology silos with application programming interfaces (APIs), and modular technology stacks that enable easy integration and connectivity with third parties.

The term "platform" has taken on a decidedly technical meaning over recent decades. This technical definition refers to an abstracted computing layer that enables rapid deployment of applications and open innovation. But today, the platform business model acts as a mechanism to organize value creation and delivery across an ecosystem of disparate systems, applications, and business partners.

For bank clients—either consumers or businesses—the platform model means a wider, richer array of products and services they can access from their primary bank, making that bank a one-stop shop with a standardized and integrated experience across multiple providers. For financial institutions it means countless more opportunities to increase their value to their clients—and their revenues, in turn—by aggregating relevant and important services.

For banks, credit unions, and other financial institutions, this is the essence of "platform strategy." Platform economics enables value creation and orchestration across a larger number of products and services **without having to build them from scratch, or having to own the assets/ resources to create them**. I emphasize that last phrase because it is at the heart of platform strategy—leveraging the capabilities, talents, and experiences of an ecosystem of trusted partners, rather than sticking with the outmoded vertical integration philosophy of building your own product portfolio from the ground up.

Let me repeat that point, because it is central to understanding the power of the platform and the benefit of platform strategy: partnerships built, nurtured and empowered through a common digital platform represent an essential transformation of how banks engage and then delight their customers, and reap the financial benefits.

We've seen this before, of course. Banking isn't the only market segment that's had to face a reckoning of business transformation brought on by platform economics. In the 1970s, IBM—by then an undisputed, often feared force in the global economy—controlled the most important segments of the information technology stack. IBM didn't just supply every class of hardware, software, and services—it developed and manufactured them internally.

This vivid example of vertical integration, combined with IBM's dominant market position, gave it unique financial and marketing power. For years, it paid off—in the form of locked-in customer ties, big profits, huge market share, and a robust and fast-growing stock price. But then came the personal computer.

In personal computing, vertical integration and customer lock-in didn't just matter less—they actually were negative forces. Built around a collaborative industry standard platform—thanks to Intel and Microsoft, and later exploited by Dell and others—the PC reshaped the IT industry's competitive landscape. After some early success, IBM quickly was outflanked by smaller OEMs that knew how to leverage the power of an industry-wide platform. The PC wars were not won by the incumbent technology suppliers but by nimble, innovative companies that understood how to exploit platform economics.

Why platform economics makes sense in banking

As I wrote with my co-authors in our 2016 book *Platform Revolution: How Networked Markets Are Transforming the Economy—And How to Make Them Work for You*, digital platforms and platform economics are changing the very nature of competition and customer experience. Platform economics has become a central part of corporate strategy in a wide range of industries outside of financial services—healthcare, technology, retail, transportation, and hospitality for instance.

There are two key factors that determine the extent to which platforms will reshape **your** industry.

The first factor is fairly easy and logical to grasp; it deals with the **extent to which the key variables of supply and demand can be digitized.** For instance, media companies did this relatively quickly and easily. They were among the first to aggressively embrace digitization for everything from content delivery and consumption to online subscriptions and streaming media for two decades. The construction industry, by comparison, has been far slower to do so. Despite the many benefits platforms provide, the industry's digital maturity has to develop further to make platform economics more widespread.

The second factor, however, though vital, is far more complex because it entails numerous sub-issues and shades of gray. It focuses on the **extent and primacy of regulation, and the cost of a failed transaction.**

The financial services industry embraced digitization early and enthusiastically, and not just for high-frequency trading and other headline-grabbing applications. The substantial volume of data being captured, both through traditional banking endpoints and through the ocean of mobile devices has created a treasure trove of insights. They can be used to create any number of personalized services—especially services a bank may not already offer, or not offer as economically as it could through a platform-based partner ecosystem.

But no one needs to be told banking is a highly regulated industry in every way from protecting customer data to filing regular, in-depth reports with regulatory bodies. Also tying into the regulatory issues, as well as the impact of failed transactions, are the twin challenges of cybersecurity and data governance—both of which have become increasingly important and challenging in banking.

What ties regulation, cybersecurity, data governance, and the high cost of failed transactions is a familiar issue: trust. Specifically, financial institutions have been hamstrung in many of their transformation efforts by an inability to create suitable, consistent, trust mechanisms. If we go on vacation and discover the rental car we tried to reserve is not available, we do at least have options. We could rent a different car or walk a few steps to the next rental car counter and start a new process to hire a new car. Here, the cost of a failed transaction for the consumer isn't very high, and while it might sting for the rental car company, it's likely a one-off experience.

But it's not that easy in financial services. In fact, the experience can range from awful, to catastrophic—if your bank-issued credit card is hacked, or your online bill payment system crashes the day your mortgage payment is due. Not only does this turn the consumer's life upside down, but it's also likely to trigger a lot of very negative implications for the bank—especially in an era of social media, when a single error can go viral, and you can become an internet meme overnight.

These are important challenges to work through and plan for when designing an Engagement Banking platform. Security, reliability, availability, and consistent user experience have to be engineered into the platform from the start and must act as the foundation for a high-trust experience.

What's driving this shift to platforms?

For hundreds of years, economists have built models, tested theories, and even built political bases around the laws of supply and demand. Whether you belong to the Adam Smith camp, or the John Maynard Keynes school, supply and demand is at the heart of modern-day economic models.

In financial services, the concept of supply and demand is changing rapidly and irrevocably. First, consider the notion of who actually owns demand for a financial product or service. No longer is it necessarily owned exclusively by a financial services company. Demand for that financial transaction could be held by a transportation company, a third-party logistics company, a hospital, or even a government agency. For the past decade, in particular, due in no small part to the creation of digital platforms, demand has slowly but steadily shifted away from vertically integrated banking channels.

At the same time, the very nature of supply itself has changed. It's increasingly likely that a consumer or commercial banking relationship is shaped and fulfilled not by a single bank, but by a web of partnerships between that bank and third-party providers of relevant services and products. These partnerships are far more common, and more necessary, as customers look for a more holistic, consolidated way to handle their financial needs. They don't want to shop for so-called "best-of-breed" financial products—retail banking here, mortgages there, business construction loans at another place. They crave—and demand—convenience, efficiency, and a unified customer experience.

The platform, with its use of APIs and open infrastructure, has made it infinitely easier, more affordable, and ultimately more profitable for banks to transform their value proposition—to move from an "everything under one roof" financial supermarket to a trusted broker of consumable services.

This links back to my earlier point regarding building trust between the bank and its customers for these third-party-provided services.

Implicit in this platform model is the understanding between buyer and seller that the bank stands by all products and services, even (and especially) when they come from third parties. Customers need to feel confident these services and their providers have been in some way tested, authenticated, and validated as to their efficacy and benefit to them. Again, using the prime contractor model—homeowners need to know a subcontractor's work is backed by the prime, and that he or she will "make it right" should any issues arise.

Where can platform strategy go from here?

I'm asked a lot about the long-term vision for platforms; whether there are new use cases around the corner... or even applications for platform-based Engagement Banking that aren't even apparent yet. One of the reasons I'm so optimistic about the role of the platform in creating more value for banks and their consumer and commercial clients is that we are only in the market's infancy. As more banks experience the "art of the possible" I'm confident they will be convening planning meetings, holding whiteboard sessions, and enacting sandbox projects to test their theories on how and where to apply platform economics next.

To understand where we will see the power of platforms in the next few years is to understand the importance—and now, the facility—of embedding financial services across a wider array of markets and experiences. There are some exciting use cases I anticipate will appear soon, even some that might not seem to make sense at first. Take gaming, for instance. Normally, it would be difficult to see a connection between banks and electronic gaming. One of the great things about gamers is they spend a ton of time online; not only are they playing games, downloading content, and chatting with friends, but they also are feverish and eager consumers of all kinds of products.

For instance, let's say someone is playing the popular Madden football game. They're not only "in the zone" when it comes to the game, but they're in the mindset for related things—like tickets to live games, team merchandise, or subscriptions to other online sports games. Platforms help the financial services provider make it easy, fast, and seamless to conduct transactions in real time. Instant gratification is a beautiful thing, and banks can help make it a reality through platforms.

Another logical extension would be the entire mortgage application process, which has become increasingly digital-first rather than walking into an office to talk with a mortgage loan officer. What if the bank handling the online mortgage application process also offered the applicant services to improve their credit score and thus attain a lower interest rate? Or scheduled an appointment with a home inspector to validate the seller's claims over their house's condition? Or lined up a contractor to repair a roof to bring it up to code before the bank would write the mortgage?

Healthcare is another area. More and more often, people have been wearing devices—or have even had sensors embedded under their skin—to monitor their health and fitness. Banking relationships with those health monitoring services also could lead to suggestions for personal training, weight-reduction centers, or physical therapy.

Small business owners also can be a ripe market segment. They not only need lines of credit for working capital, or to fuel expansion, but also consume essential services such as legal, accounting, marketing, and compliance. The platform enables financial services to assemble an all-star team of complementary service providers working together on behalf of that business. Not only does the small business owner become even more engaged with their bank as the nexus for those business services, but undoubtedly the bank can develop a referral fee schedule to generate incremental revenue while serving the customer.

The whole idea is to embed financial services—the secondary demand—closer to the decision they enable—the primary demand—and platforms make that happen. For banks, the economic benefits can be substantial; incremental revenue, often with high-profit repeat customers, without huge investments in marketing programs or hiring dedicated sales professionals.

Action steps for banking leaders

Now we've addressed how platform strategy works, how it benefits both sellers and buyers, and what future opportunities look like, let's bring it back to a here-and-now context: what can—and should—banking executives do to leverage the platform model for increased client engagement and improved financial outcomes?

On pages 39 and 40 you'll find action steps which banking leaders should take and involve their organizations in. No one should expect this to be a set-and-forget kind of process. It takes thoughtful planning, careful execution, and honest assessment of what is working and what isn't; and issues are likely to arise that might not have been anticipated at the front end.

The banks most likely to succeed in the future, in the face of what will surely be momentous changes in technology and customer requirements, will be the ones that build the most robust, flexible, and open platforms.

1. "Bank Customer Loyalty Declining: 47 Percent of U.S. Consumers Would Consider Target or Walmart as a Banking Alternative", Businesswire, April 19, 2016, https://www.businesswire.com/news/home/20160419005137/en/Bank-Customer-Loyalty-Declining-47-Percent-of-U.S.-Consumers-Would-Consider-Target-or-Walmart-as-a-Banking-Alternative
2. "Banking's Amazon Moment", Bain & Company, March 05, 2019, https://www.bain.com/insights/bankings-amazon-moment/

Action steps for banking leaders

Innovate embedded products and services

Think about your products and services as modular components that can be integrated and deeply embedded into different contexts. Banking leaders should challenge themselves and their organization to think about how their solutions can become essential elements in everyday life. Think about it in the context of transportation, or retail, or business services for example. This should replace legacy thinking about banking channels, such as neighborhood branches, retail pop-up kiosks, online banking or mobile transactions.

Create open loop ecosystems

Avoid emulating the tech giants like Facebook, Google, or Amazon. They all have created expansive yet closed-loop models like app stores or marketplaces. While these have served them well, they were created at a time when locking customers into a closed loop ecosystem was standard operating procedure. We are unlikely to see such closed loop models dominate financial services. Customers make financial decisions across a variety of interfaces and financial services will have to be embedded across an increasingly fragmented set of interfaces.

Action steps for banking leaders (continued)

Use agile technology infrastructure

Platforms do not work in a siloed environment. Technology silos, as well as workflow silos, prevent your platform from fast, nimble, and flexible scaling. While your infrastructure may need to be modernized to better leverage APIs, the smarter way to go is to wrap a layer around your existing technology stack and expose your services through those APIs. This helps to create a standardized mechanism to define, develop, and deploy your internal capabilities throughout your expansive partner ecosystem. While some banking C-suite executives may be more comfortable leaving the infrastructure decisions to their CIO or CTO, it's a strategic consideration in which the C-suite and the Board need to be involved.

Embrace standardization and integration

Finally, embrace standardization and integration for the massive amounts of data your platform will collect. Capturing, storing, sharing, analyzing, and purposing data coming from multiple, often incompatible systems can be incredibly complex, frustrating, and expensive without standards. This will also make your partner transactions on your platform far more economical and secure, as well as faster.

Chapter 3

The Engagement Banking revolution

Jouk Pleiter, Founder and Chief Executive Officer, Backbase

The Engagement Banking revolution is happening.

You can't stop it. You can't even slow it down. It will happen whether you choose to participate or not. And it will happen quickly. It's a movie we've seen many times in the first two decades of this century: telecommunications, shopping, transportation, music, advertising, media, home entertainment, hospitality, photography. All disrupted; all changed; all revolutionized.

You think "revolution" is too strong a term? Try telling that to the CEOs of Borders, or Tower Records, or Toys 'R Us; or of hundreds of defunct newspapers, magazines, local book stores . . .

You can't, of course. Because those companies no longer exist.

Do you think banking is somehow immune, perhaps because it hasn't yet been as deeply affected as some other industries? Or perhaps because it is highly regulated, or because customers are afraid to end long-standing relationships? Or perhaps because banking has been slow to evolve due to highly interconnected processes and technologies for payments, processing, and other business activities?

Well, those issues still exist, but they no longer mitigate the impact of similar disruption in banking.

But why not? And why is the banking industry barreling down an inexorable, intractable, and inevitable path of revolution?

It would be simple to say it's all about technology. And technology is, of course, the primary catalyst. Were it not for digital and mobile technology, we would not be talking about revolution; just complacently moving forward in a ho-hum business-as-usual attitude. But if you think it's **just** about the technology, you risk missing the crux of what the revolution in banking **is** all about.

The revolution in banking is really all about **the customer.**

Whatever their profile—an individual, a family, a small business, a large enterprise; local, regional, multi-national, or global—our customers are now calling the shots in ways they have never been able to before. Good for them. And if we are willing to listen to them, lead them, innovate for them, and give them what they want and need, good for us as well.

The customer-centric viewpoint is the "Engagement" factor in the Engagement Banking revolution. It's why I am writing this chapter, and hopefully why you are reading this book. But what is true customer engagement? What does it look and feel like in banking? How do we evolve our organizations and operating models to be embodied by engagement in everything we do? Is it possible to become a bank that people love?

The possibility for exponential change

As we've seen over the past 20 years or so, digital disruption takes place in an industry when new competitors—typically digital-native startups—innovate with a new business or operating model that offers customers a 10x improvement in experience. They use technology to eliminate friction and engage customers in ways never before possible. Iconic examples are technologies such as the iPhone and companies such as Uber, Airbnb, and Amazon.

Established companies and traditional leaders are often blindsided by these new business models. They become locked in with monolithic IT infrastructures and operating models that make it difficult, if not impossible, to react as quickly, decisively, and extensively as needed to participate in the disruption. That is, if their leaders are even prescient enough to see the writing on the wall.

If your bank is like most others, the impact of digital disruption is already affecting your bottom line, and in all likelihood is beginning to test your relationships with your customers—and their loyalty to your bank and brand. Customers are judging you by your convenience factor, and if they are not satisfied they will vote with their feet.

In just about every product or service you offer, customers can now turn to a digital-native alternative that gives them that disruption-defining 10x improvement in engagement: payments, credit, financial advice, wealth management, mortgages, loans. When customers love using their apps, they use them all the time. They want to access them anytime, using any device, any channel, from any location. They want an experience that is fast, intuitive, secure, friction-free, satisfying, fulfilling, and yes, sometimes even fun, enlightening, or pleasantly surprising.

The power of the platform

These engaging new digital products and services come from three primary non-traditional, digital-native sources: the FinTechs, the Neobanks, and the Big Techs—such as Apple, Google, Microsoft, and Amazon. Until the banks of the present join the revolution, these organizations have their sights (and sites) set on becoming the banks of the future.

Digital and mobile technologies provide the foundation upon which the FinTechs, Neobanks, and Big Techs are disrupting the banking industry. But what transforms that disruption into revolution is an ability to leverage a platform model to accelerate, expand, and unify services; and infuse them with automation, rich data, intelligence, analytics, and agility.

The platform model is the game-changer for the FinTechs, Neobanks, and Big Techs. They can start with a single product or service, build a relationship with the customer, gain insight into what makes the customer tick, and then easily add new features and capabilities until that single service eventually becomes a full portfolio.

From the customer's perspective, it's a seamless, friction-free journey—
Apple Pay leads to Apple Card leads to Apple Wallet leads to... what's
next? Apple Savings, Apple Loan, Apple Mortgage, and Apple Wealth
Management? Apple Financial Services? Actually, that one already exists.

From the perspective of traditional banks—and that might include
yours—it's a particularly pernicious model when used by a digital-native
competitor because it takes away pieces of the business a bit at a time.
Until all of a sudden, what you thought was your business model is no
longer your business model, and who you thought was your customer is no
longer your customer.

Some banks have already seen there's a better alternative. Barclays
switched to looking at their eight million customers and merchants as
their biggest assets, rather than liabilities; it's changed how they run their
organization.[1] We've also seen other banks transform user experience via
an Engagement Banking platform architected around the customer. Not
just tilting it in their favor, but rocketing app engagement from 40% to
90%. Results even some Big Techs can only aspire to.[2]

The opportunity is there for your taking. But as we've seen in so many
other industries, once customers have expanded choices they trust, and
access to that 10x experience, they move quickly and without much regard
for brand loyalty—or nostalgia for the way things have always been done.

The vision: becoming a bank people love

So, how does your bank evolve from its current state into a bank people love?

The best way to start —or perhaps the only way—is to put yourself in the customer's seat. Look at your customers as individuals. How will you make their lives easier? How will you make them feel happy and secure? What do they want? What do they need? What will create a friction-free experience? What will make them so enthused they'll want to tell their families and friends?

Don't worry about what it will take to get there; instead, think about what it will look like once you arrive at your destination. If you know where you are going, you can figure out what it will take to make the journey. If you don't know where you are going, you are likely to lose your way.

So, let's begin with the ending.

Imagine the revolution is over. There is a new way of banking, of engaging with customers, of continuing to evolve with customers as their needs and desires continuously change. It's fueled by new technologies, new demands, new ideas, and new innovations.

What does that world look like? What does your bank look like?

It looks like this:

Your bank has become an engagement hub.

It's more than just the place your customers go for their financial transactions — it's now an essential part of their daily lives. They can log in from any device with ease, but not just to bank; they use your app to buy a suitcase, order flowers, book a ski trip, access discounts, manage budgets, monitor their investments, and more. They can put their phones in their pockets, safe and assured in the knowledge that if there is a financial decision to be made, your bank will either make it and take the appropriate action, or send them a reminder, replete with all the details they need and all the options available.

More importantly, your relationship with your customer has shifted in a fundamental way. You're the Alfred to their Batman. You grow with them over the course of their lives; and through AI-powered capabilities, you're able to provide them the exact service or recommend just the right products they need at every pivotal moment and milestone they experience. Whether they're getting married, or buying their first home, or expanding their business internationally—your bank is right there with them.

The trust they have in your bank is only rivaled by their loyalty to it. They feel deeply assured that they're in the hands of a digital partner whose every action and decision is architected around their very specific, very personal needs. They sense—to a degree they've never previously experienced—that their financial wellbeing is taken care of. They are happy and they love the convenience, confidence, and personalized care your bank provides.

Now: how do you get there from here?

How do you make sure you're focused on your customers—your every customer—as ultimate beneficiaries? How do you create an engagement-first strategy that is completely your own; one that fits your unique digital transformation, allowing you to stand out from your competitors? How do you reach a 10x improvement in customer experience which will transform yours into a bank people love? And once you've achieved that, how do you make sure you can sustain it?

The path to fulfilling your vision of your bank as the single engagement hub for your customers is surprisingly clear—and probably a lot simpler than you think.

Your mission: Re-architecting banking around the customer

It begins with you recognizing it's no longer practical or feasible to continue to try to use your existing systems of record for customer engagement. Those systems were designed around your bank and its products—not customers. Typically, such systems are monolithic and inflexible—built to run enterprise-level applications with reliability and stability. But that's actually a positive: you **need** reliability and stability in your systems of record. Changing those systems every time you come up with an innovative idea would be a nightmare. Even if you wanted to, you couldn't do it without significant downtime, causing disruption and dismay for your employees and customers.

But being unable to drive innovation with your existing systems of record **doesn't** mean you can't drive innovation at all—or that those systems won't be critical and fundamental to your next-generation platform-based approach. In fact, because your systems of record hold a large percentage of your most valuable customer data, they'll form a vital tier in whatever innovation you drive. The data just needs to be unlocked.

To achieve the innovation, speed, and customer engagement that's essential to compete in today's environment, your bank must evolve to a new model. A model that seamlessly integrates with, builds upon, and complements your systems of record without forcing you to make major changes to them.

What does that new model look like?

Several years ago the consulting firm McKinsey & Company articulated a vision for a two-speed IT architecture.[3] The concept was to deploy a fast-speed, customer-centric front end running alongside a slow-speed, transaction-focused legacy back end. As McKinsey described it:

> *For software release cycles and deployment mechanisms, the customer-facing part should be modular, to enable quick deployment of new software by avoiding time-consuming integration work. In contrast, the transactional existing systems of record must be designed for stability and high-quality data management, which leads to longer release cycles.*

This model could be used by many incumbent banks of today to provide a simple and elegant, innovation-empowering path to the future. **Your** bank could be one of them. You **can** achieve positive disruption to your business models without causing negative disruption to your existing systems and technologies.

In the banking model of a two-speed IT architecture, the slow-speed systems of record don't undergo any major changes. They are loosely coupled with a system of engagement layer that sits atop them, seamlessly and complimentarily interacting with them to both deliver and access business-critical and customer-critical data and applications.

This two-speed approach will enable your bank to evolve to an outside-in model of engagement, providing the speed and flexibility it will need to react quickly and decisively to customer needs as they arise. It will empower you to capture a new "heartbeat of innovation". The unprecedented development speed it will provide may feel jolting at first—but this initial jolt will prove a powerful, long-term catalyst for transformative change for your business, your employees, and, most importantly, your customers.

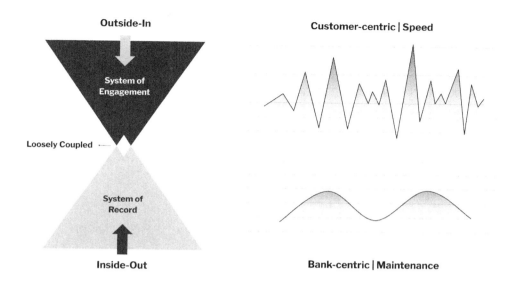

Figure 1: Systems of Engagement vs. Systems of Record—a loosely coupled architecture for innovation. Source: Backbase

In addition to enabling your bank's evolution to an outside-in, customer-centric model for innovation, this modern approach will empower it to finally shift its customer engagement from being defined by vertical silos to being defined by a horizontal platform.

This will allow you to engage with your customers on **their** terms. You'll be able to organize your engagement in ways your customers will relate to, based on the vast array of services they can leverage from your organization—core banking, loans, mortgages, payments, fintech, and others—rather than within the limits of your existing systems of record.

I mentioned earlier that evolving to this new model is probably easier than you think. That's because you don't have to change your monolithic systems. Nor do you have to deal with the downtime and disruption that might cause. Rather, you can and should focus on loosely coupling the right engagement layer atop your systems of record.

The way to capture and sustain this new heartbeat of innovation is by focusing on **owning your engagement layer**.

An engagement layer, however, is people-focused by design, as opposed to process-focused. It overlays and complements your core system, and gives you a flexible, low-friction pathway towards delivering exceptional digital tools and experiences for your customers and employees. This is where you'll be able to truly differentiate from your competitors by reimagining what the banking experience could be like.

The reason I suggest the path is probably simpler than you think is that owning the engagement layer means committing to a single platform approach. If you use the right platform, you'll be able to orchestrate all customer touchpoints in one place, with one consistent approach. Once you've chosen your engagement platform, your journey to the future will become clear and relatively straightforward. Your engagement platform will be a hub from which you'll orchestrate all your customers' needs: your own applications and services; your own partner services; and any other software-as-a-service, third-party solutions your customers choose to use.

Let me emphasize that last part: solutions your customers choose to use... That is what architecting around your customers is truly about. It's not about how you can sell them more products or force them to choose the partners or services you prefer. It's about giving them the opportunity to make their own choices; to make the decisions that are best for them.

Your bank will be the hub of a broad financial ecosystem, with your customers at the helm of their own destinies. By taking control of the system of engagement, you will reduce friction, put the customer in control, and achieve that 10x improvement in customer experience that will thrill your customers and earn their loyalty, passion, commitment, and respect.

Customer-first engagement-everything is the way forward: the path to acquiring and inspiring new customers, innovating with new forms of engagement, and creating new expectations and measurements of customer loyalty. It is the foundation for your next-generation initiatives—whether their focus is onboarding, self-servicing, driving loyalty, growing share of wallet through loan origination, or something else you deem engaging for your customers and organization.

Overcoming the challenges faced by traditional banks

The disruption in banking is taking place right now, right before our eyes. Many banking executives and leaders will feel a strong sense of urgency to get moving as fast as possible. They're right to feel that. In this case the pressure to move fast is a good thing—for several reasons.

First, as noted, the competition is already well defined and out there giving customers the 10x improvement in engagement and experience that the revolution is all about. In Germany, 84% of existing online banking users would like to be able to request and purchase additional banking products in a simple digital way.[4] You should anticipate your customer's needs, innovate, and deliver new products and services intuitively. If you don't? Well, customers are already going elsewhere for better experiences.

Second, the pandemic has changed the rules and rapidly accelerated the need for digital transformation in banking. Over the past two-years, people have become much more dependent, comfortable, and secure with their online and mobile interactions. The pandemic made them see the proverbial light—and that light is a digital one. In Japan, 25% of consumers report using digital banking more often now than they did before the pandemic. This has had a direct impact on Japanese banks' priorities and strategies: 74% of Japanese banks and securities firms reported the pandemic acted as a catalyst to accelerating their digital transformations.[5]

Banking isn't going back to the way it was. Ever.

But... just because there's urgency to join the revolution, it doesn't mean you should panic. Move fast, yes; but with a well-considered plan and strategy in place. The first step is an honest assessment of where your bank is, and what obstacles lie in the way of it executing the digital transformation necessary to secure its future. If yours is like most banks, there will be four or five key obstacles pinpointed by that assessment.

So: how do you (quickly) overcome those obstacles to ensure your bank will not only survive the disruption, but also emerge as a leader—and a bank people love?

Let's look at each obstacle and how to overcome it.

People

This is a new era. It requires new skills. Your bank will have to function as a platform-native institution, so it's important that you have platform and digital natives on your teams. You'll need individuals with expertise in cloud computing; agile development; DevOps; microservices; containers; APIs; cybersecurity... and all other aspects of a modern cloud- and digital-native technology platform.

You will rightfully note people with many of these skills are hard to come by and keep—there always being such high demand for qualified talent. This makes it extremely important to have the right leadership to guide your digital transformation efforts. It may be more cost-efficient—and fundamentally more successful—to expand your partner ecosystem and leverage their knowledge and expertise. After all, a company that manages to keep great people to build their own high-usage products is just the kind you want to partner with to benefit your Engagement Banking platform.

Inefficient legacy technology

Existing banking backend infrastructures were designed for a different era. Typically they have not kept up with the pace of change. Your IT department may have been able to modernize certain applications and bring some channel innovation into your bank's picture, but it won't be enough.

To compete in an increasingly disrupted market, banks need to modernize—but without replacing the existing systems of record they've invested in, and still depend upon. This means embracing cloud computing; eliminating silos; eliminating duplication; and ensuring backends and systems of record can work seamlessly and friction-free with next-generation Engagement Banking platforms.

As your bank continues to innovate and create new business models, it will need technology that **enables** innovation far into the future—not technology that will restrict it.

Disconnected channels

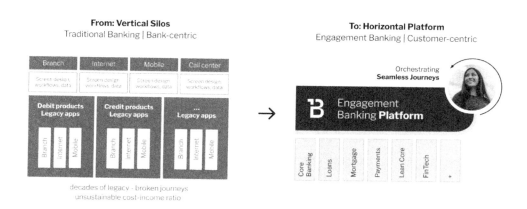

Figure 2: Customer-centric Engagement Banking to eradicate silos. Source: Backbase

As more digital touchpoints have been added—for call centers, online and web services, and—with the introduction of smartphones—for mobile apps and services, these services are typically in silos as a result of being tacked on to existing systems of record. When they're not connected to one another, they're not capable of giving the bank a single, holistic view of the customer. Nor can they give customers a single, holistic, data-driven experience across all channels. By loosely coupling an Engagement Banking platform onto existing systems of record, you can achieve friction-free 10x improvement and eradicating silos (see Figure 2). Offering such an improvement across all channels, seamlessly, and with consistent, unified data and applications, must be a top priority for your bank.

Obsolete operating models

Legacy operating models in banks are based on inefficient legacy technology platforms, siloed channels, and obsolete notions. Like the notion that banks understand exactly what their customers really want and need because they have long-standing relationships with them.

Such mistakes are unfortunately common among established companies—making them particularly vulnerable to disruption. The late Clayton Christenson, Harvard Business School Professor, consultant and management guru, described some of these challenges in his seminal work on disruptive innovation. Christensen warned of the dangers of large established companies becoming **too** good at what they do best.[6]

The basic concept is that established companies tend to develop products to satisfy the demands of their most sophisticated customers, which can make them blind to the needs of **less** sophisticated customers—who may eventually form much larger markets. An upstart can therefore introduce a simpler product more targeted to changing customer needs. Through incremental innovation, such products can be refined and moved upmarket, completing the disruption of the original company.

In banking, operating models tend to be focused on an inside-out model, whereby banks develop the products and services they think customers want and need. The Engagement Banking revolution inverts that, by necessity—and shifts to an **outside-in** model, whereby customers dictate the products and services they need, and banks become central hubs for delivering those services.

With an engagement platform, a bank not only has the facilities to listen to, and gain from, ongoing customer feedback in a continuous development loop, but can also anticipate customer needs and build new solutions that offer customer-delighting features. Even features beyond what customers could have imagined.

To take advantage of the possibilities of new generation technologies—such as artificial intelligence, augmented reality, virtual reality, blockchain, and other innovations, your bank must have a proactive, anticipatory platform model: designed to facilitate and accelerate change.

Culture

Broadening your ecosystem and being open to hiring younger, more digital-native people is an extension of the disruption you will probably need to make in your cultures. The old ways of doing things won't work anymore. Your branches will take on less importance in building customer relationships and engagement.

People will still be essential, but more and more frequently customers will judge you on the quality of their digital experience. But banking cultures tend to be conservative, risk averse, and slow. The idea of revolution is anathema to what banking executives and Boards would ever claim they want. Just as I'm sure it was anathema for the executives and Boards in publishing, advertising, and media who didn't respond to the digital needs and expectations of their customers.

I am confident that you—the Boards and executives reading this book—know you must adjust and evolve. That you understand you have to let go of the old ways. After all, that is why you are reading this book—to understand how you can make those changes now.

The path forward

As we've seen across every digitally disrupted industry, the platform model is the key to delivering the speed, agility, innovation, and engagement that delights customers and delivers that exponential 10x improvement in customer experience. But not only does the platform model deliver what customers are looking for; it also shows them there's a better way. The way the customer engages with the ecosystem and derives value from it is what makes each platform different, and **unique** to the company providing it—thereby turning customers into lifelong fans.

That's why banks are trying to figure out how to become more engaged with their customers. And what to **do** to ensure they own their engagement layer through an Engagement Banking platform will be one of the most critical decisions banking executives will ever need to make.

From an Engagement Banking platform perspective, there are several options to consider. But the most obviously apparent options seem to make it a binary decision—whether to build your own, or work with a partner to acquire one.

However, this decision is not quite as binary as it may seem. If you commit to a pure "build-your-own" model, you are basically making a decision to become a software/technology company. Think how many years it's taken Big Tech and FinTech to develop their products. They have established brands which they use to recruit and retain the hundreds, if not thousands, of IT and digital people necessary to build, operate, manage, and scale a huge operation. Trying to do that from scratch is a mammoth task, especially given you'll be competing against them—and masses of other companies—within the same small talent-pool.

The Big Techs and FinTechs will have spent the majority of their time building the basics—a login button, security, protection of data, and how they access their accounts.

Why would you build it yourself, when you can partner with companies who know how to do it, and have already built more than just the basics?

Banks will need to modernize their legacy IT infrastructures and existing systems of record to deliver their Engagement Banking platforms. That could be daunting. It may also be wasteful, particularly if they follow a path that doesn't protect their existing investments. Alternatively, there are existing platforms that provide the fast, powerful infrastructure necessary for computing, storage, and networks; and a migration to cloud and cloud-native development whenever and wherever possible. There are also platforms that are pre-integrated to work with existing systems of record through a cloud-native core. These platforms allow banks to empower their developers to build custom apps, while adopting out-of-the-box applications to deliver innovation at scale.

Your bank's Engagement Banking platform should be its digital hub in which everything comes together. It should be integrated, aggregated, omnichannel, open, data-driven, fast, agile, modular, and proactive. It should be the driver of your bank's intelligence, analytics, and innovation. It should be where, when, and how your bank's customer engagement is orchestrated—now, and into the future.

The Engagement Banking platform

I want to clarify what your Engagement Banking platform should look like, what kind of functionality it should deliver, and the massive investment in technology that will be required to deliver that functionality.

As shown in Figure 3, your Engagement Banking platform will be the engine room of your engagement layer. It should be loosely coupled with your systems of record to leverage APIs, cloud technologies, microservices, and other modern tools to deliver broad functionality and agility—along with seamless integration with your existing systems of record. An Engagement Banking platform is horizontal rather than vertical, and has two speeds rather than one.

	API	API	API	API	API	API	+
Onboarding & Lending	Workflow	Case Mngt	KYC / AML	Decisioning	Track & Trace	Documents	+
Daily Banking	Accounts	Transactions	Payments	Cards	Insights	Stock / Crypto	+
Engagement Orchestration	Notify / Alert	Nudges	Audience	Campaigns	Video / Voice	Chat	+
Identity, Access & Entitlements Mngt	User Mngt	Access Control	Entitlements	Authy / Verify	Device Mngt	Audit	+
Developer Enablement	API	SDK	Design System	Stream	Backbase.io	AI/ML	+
Cloud & DevOps	Provisioning	Monitoring	Compliance	Security	Incident Mngt	DevOps	+

Figure 3: Engagement Banking Platform—the engine room of your engagement layer.
Source: Backbase

The simplicity by which you can acquire ownership of your engagement layer by partnering with a platform company is not indicative of how substantial that layer might be. It's only through spending many thousands, and thousands of person days on building, refining, and innovating that our company, Backbase, has been able to deliver a best-in-class Engagement Banking platform. It's a daunting vision that has come to life after more than a decade's worth of work by thousands of engineers. Although I am quite proud of our work, I mention this not to be boastful, but to ensure that you are mindful of the kind of commitment and investment involved in tackling such an endeavor.

Also, remember this point: the fact that Engagement Banking platforms are simple to deploy and use by design doesn't mean they're not complex and difficult to build. In fact, the simplicity of the architecture involved requires an enormous amount of technological savvy, experience, time, knowledge, and innovation to pull off. And it is a process that never ends.

We are continuously iterating the Engagement Banking platform to simplify the delivery of seamless customer journeys, as you can see in the illustration below.

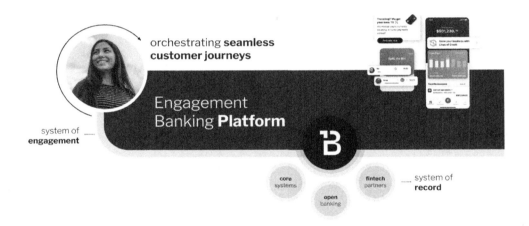

Figure 4: The Engagement Banking Platform. Source: Backbase

This approach delivers the two-speed, outside-in model I described previously in this chapter. In terms of developing new solutions and driving the heartbeat of innovation, it makes the build or buy decision nonbinary by giving banks the flexibility to build custom applications and/or use proven out-of-the-box solutions. With this approach, you can **adopt and build and** go as fast as you need to go on product development and innovation, assured that your apps will work seamlessly with both your Engagement Banking platform **and** your systems of record.

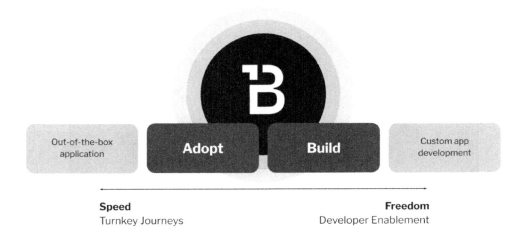

Figure 5: The Unique Differentiator. Source: Backbase

Rearchitecting banking around the customer means putting the customer at the center of everything you do, delivering seamless journeys—all powered by one single platform—your Engagement Banking Platform of choice.

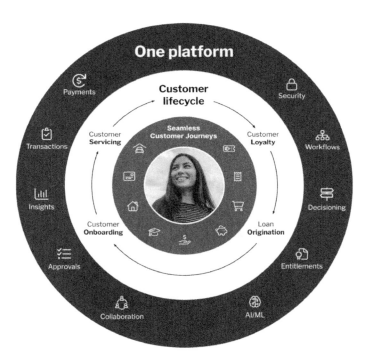

Figure 6: Engagement Banking platform. Source: Backbase

How you choose to structure the Engagement Banking platform within your environment is best based on what you think will work for your teams and cultures.

Some banks choose to integrate the Engagement Banking platform into their existing structure and move the entire bank towards a new operating model, undergoing wholesale change executed one step at a time. Others choose to create their own Neobank—which they operate as a new, separate entity cannibalizing their traditional business—rather than lose that business and its customers to a competitor.

Regardless of how you choose to move forward, the platform you use must be cloud-based with a modern, open technology foundation. Overall, the key is to make sure you are using an Engagement Banking platform that starts with a philosophy of integrating your IT infrastructure layer with your engagement layer and providing an open platform. These are the foundational elements that will let your organization aggregate all data and information to deliver a fully engaged, fully orchestrated, future-proofed customer experience.

Looking ahead

If you are a banking leader or executive—whether you sit on the Board, or in the IT or digital department, or anywhere else—it's time you realized this is no time for complacency or inaction. The legacy banking models of the past are over; done, finished, kaput. They will no longer work for your organization; and more importantly, they will no longer work for your current or future customers.

It is time to modernize your bank's technology and business processes, leaving behind the world in which data and operations are siloed; where legacy infrastructure is not connected to cloud models; where progress is measured in increments, stifled by "Waterfall" development processes that take years; where your bank took on technology modernization single-handedly as a burden, rather than as a golden opportunity to work with partners to help it spark engagement and inspire innovation.

Yesterday's world is gone. Tomorrow's world is open, unified, fast, engaging. It is a breeding ground for innovation. It is a path to create new experiences that customers will love—precisely because they will welcome engagement that will change their lives for the better and enable them to reimagine their relationship with banking and finance. Most importantly, tomorrow's world is built on a single platform approach: the Engagement Banking platform. I'm describing it as "tomorrow's world" but in reality, it is happening today. Right now.

As I said at the beginning of this chapter, you can't stop the Engagement Banking revolution. You can't even slow it down. Your competitors—FinTechs, Neobanks, and Big Techs—are agile, adept, and aggressive. They know how to use platform models to disrupt industries, and they are using them to disrupt banking. **Right now.**

It is time to fight fire with fire—or, to be less hyperbolic and more precise—to fight their platforms with a platform of your own. You can build one, or you can use one specifically designed to meet the needs of digital transformation for traditional banks, credit unions, and other financial institutions.

How you choose to move forward is up to you. Standing still is not an option.

The Engagement Banking revolution has **begun.**

1. "The Platform Era Unfolds", The MIT Initiative on the digital economy, August, 2019, https://ide.mit.edu/insights/the-platform-era-unfolds/
2. "Jouk Pleiter keynote presentation: Engage 2022", Backbase, November, 2021, https://fast.wistia.net/embed/channel/355q8nsxx8?wchannelid=355q8nsxx8&wvideoid=fjphcgshw9
3. "A two-speed IT architecture for the digital enterprise", McKinsey & Company, December, 2014, https://www.mckinsey.com/business-functions/mckinsey-digital/our-insights/a-two-speed-it-architecture-for-the-digital-enterprise
4. "Study shows growing gap between German customer expectations and digital banking offerings", Backbase, November, 2021
5. "The future of digital banking in Japan", Forrester Consulting, October, 2021
6. "The Essential Clayton Christensen Articles", Harvard Business Review, January 24, 2020, https://hbr.org/2020/01/the-essential-clayton-christensen-articles

How to transform your bank

Chapter 4

The path to business model innovation

Paolo Sironi, Author; Global Research Leader,
Banking and Financial Markets, IBM

What do crop worms, taxi bookings, and online shopping have to do with banking?

In today's environment, what banking is about—and what it does—are increasingly in the eye of the beholder.

DBS Bank in Singapore was an earlier adopter of digital banking, investing heavily in the end-to-end hyper-digitalization of its operations. As a result, the bank launched a comprehensive API development platform and focused on creating distinct marketplaces, leveraging non-banking partners to change and adapt its business models. Beginning in 2017, DBS Bank has started a car marketplace, a platform solution for electricity contracts, a real estate digital play, and a travel solution.

Bank of Baroda is a community bank in India with a customer base heavily involved in farming and agriculture. In 2019, the bank launched "Baroda Kisan," an agri-digital marketplace designed to cater to farmers' non-banking needs. It provides weather forecasts, crop conditions, updates on the moisture levels of the soil, market prices, special crop-related consultation, and of course information on crop worms.

The State Bank of India is the largest bank in India with more than 350 million customers—more than the entire population of the United States. In 2017, it launched a digital app named "You Only Need One." YONO, as it is called, was designed to enable customers to access an e-commerce platform underpinned by a digital wallet and, of course, a variety of financial services. In just five years, YONO's services—and customer engagement—grew so substantially that in 2021, SBI Chairman Rajnish Kumar estimated YONO's market valuation would be equal to that of SBI, if not larger.[1]

Evidently, banks all over the world are beholding new opportunities to leverage digital platform models to expand their reach—in ways that would have been both impossible and implausible as recently as 2010.

Take the Bank of Baroda model. Yes, the platform provides specialized information about crop worms. It also provides a wide range of what would be considered "known" banking services—such as a digital wallet, innovative financing options for purchasing or renting equipment, and more.

Or the DBS Car Marketplace. It isn't just a digital site to find new or used cars—it's also a platform that aims to facilitate transactions consisting of leasing, insurance, and credit card applications.

Welcome to the future of banking—the age of platform economies and the Engagement Banking revolution.

In this new world, banks are able to create new business models that derive a higher-level value than they have previously achieved in customer engagements. These include:

1. **Transparent services** that uncover **hidden value** in client engagements, based on trusted advisory relationships.

2. **Embedded services** that create **new value** in customer engagements, from sources that are typically net new for banks to deliver to users.

Banks now have an opportunity to surface both hidden and new value and drive that value to the bottom line in the way of new revenue streams, through enhanced, data-driven, intelligence-based customer relationships. This represents a new way of thinking about banking—what it can be and where it is going.

But something fundamental has to pivot in entrepreneurial and corporate mindsets.

Traditionally, banking business models have been product focused, with the intent to deliver certain results measured in the quantification of **outputs**, such as discrete sales figures or quantities. Revenues have been typically based on selling more products or capturing interest rate margins. This business architecture is no longer able to stand the test of time and is facing an accelerated shift towards new economic, social, and digital norms.

To generate business value for now and the future, banks need a new strategic anchor focused not on outputs, but on **outcomes.** In this paradigm, the main economic levers lie in the ability of new business models to engage users continuously through digital technology. Increasingly, revenues are derived through transparent and embedded services that customers find valuable and helpful—and eventually view as essential.

Innovators are required to think in a non-linear manner through novel, data-driven, and continuously communicated understanding of user needs. It is through the transparent usage of digital technologies and platform delivery models that organizations can win users' trust and deliver the friction-free, engaging experiences that capture loyalty and foster ongoing business relationships.

This shift to what I call **"outcome economies"** is a tsunami for traditional business culture. In this chapter I explore what is required for banking and financial services to evolve and innovate new business models. I also provide practical guidance on how banking leaders can generate sustainable, high-level business value as they embrace digital transformation, platform economies, and Engagement Banking.

Seeing the humanity of clients

In other chapters throughout this book, experts sing from the same hymnbook of putting the client at the center of the business. In my view, client-centricity means: **empowering clients to become active users of transparent digital services to achieve their personal, professional, and financial goals.**

I find it helpful to overcome the traditional view of a "passive client"—to whom you can sell more stuff—and shift to a more inclusive perspective of viewing the customer as an "active human being" with personal needs and desires. For a bank to become one that people trust, it's important to understand the value of adjusting business models to put humans—not products or transactions—at the real center of the engagement model. From that point on, it suddenly becomes much easier to broaden, and even reimagine, the value of the engagements being offered to the human user.

Some forward-looking institutions have already seen the light.

On the one side, they've started by embedding financial services inside non-banking journeys to expand the relevance of their offerings. This required new design thinking processes, taken from the needs of clients—as opposed to the traditional perspective of bankers. The outcome was the rewiring of client engagement by contextualizing the customer relationship inside non-banking digital platforms. **It is the opportunity to eliminate the friction in client engagements that makes banking contextual, and that is embedded to unlock new value at the intersection of multiple industries. This platform strategy is called "Contextual Banking".**

On the other side, early adopters of platform technologies also recognized the benefits of becoming centers of competencies and advisory services to support customers in their journeys to plan and achieve their goals. Centering relationships means bundling banking offers in an "all-in" solution that provides trusted advice, supported by a digital framework to address financial well-being for the people who are consuming your services.

In a banking world in which clients pay not for financial products but for the services they consume, low-margin credit origination acquires new value, as it becomes the core of the personalization process of the advisory platform. The liabilities of families and firms are all different, while the assets available in the market tend to commoditize, whether they are liquid or illiquid.

Therefore, blurring the borders dividing lines of business in financial services, and flipping their relative relevance with respect to interest rate margins and fee businesses, is allowing banks to find new rewards for core banking operations inside financial planning and advisory services. This is a relevant pillar of value demonstration, as clients are progressively being asked to pay transparently for platform access—and for any relationships, human or digital, outside product transactions (e.g. fees on top). **It is the need to demonstrate value that makes banking conscious, or transparent, to unlock hidden value inside financial relationships. This platform strategy is called "Conscious Banking."**

The industry is witnessing this progressive transformation of business strategies, as banks shift their focus from interest rates margins to the intermediation of products and services. For example, in 2020, FTSE Russel dropped the largest Swiss bank from the STOXX banking index, classifying UBS as an Asset Management company.[2] This reflected the evolution of the Swiss lender toward an "all-in" business strategy, which is centered on more affordable and holistic wealth management relationships underpinned by new profitability models based on client fees instead of product sales.

Put into the context of Engagement Banking: Contextual Banking is the engagement layer that enables banks to own the frictionless engagements the human user has within the ecosystem. Conscious Banking is the hidden value within the ecosystem and the engagements delivered through an advisory platform.

Introducing the Banking Reinvention Quadrant

This existential transformation of bank business models toward Contextual Banking and Conscious Banking is driven by the impact of the monetary and economic conditions in which banks operate globally—the soaring cost of capital; the increased transparency on costs and conflicts of interests; and the progressive commoditization of financial products. Digital technology is not the primary reason for business change. It is the accelerator. But it's not just accelerating innovation for traditional banks; it is accelerating innovation—and potential disruption—across the entire financial services industry.

On the one hand, the pandemic crisis pushed consumers to adapt to a digital-first world, increasing the acceptance of digital touch-points following governments' demand for social distancing. On the other hand, digital technology accelerated the entry of specialized providers chipping away at banking activities that do not require access to a large balance sheet, such as payments and wealth management.

Similarly, digital platforms have interjected themselves between banks and customers, potentially monopolizing access to valuable data. As a result, banks risk losing their position as "first point of contact" for financial services and could be reduced to becoming merely upstream suppliers of maturity transformation services that have no direct customer access.

To avoid being displaced and disrupted, banks must adapt to this changing environment and achieve high-value interactions and touch points with customers, with a growing emphasis on transparent interactions and embedded services to derive new value.

How do banks transform from current business models to new high-value digital business models?

For this we turn to the Banking Reinvention Quadrant (BRQ) (see Figure 1), which I have created as a visual representation of the strategies needed to succeed in the existential evolution of bank business models.

Ultimately, changing a business model means changing the way banks monetize banking and non-banking relationships—with their clients and across all platform users in adjacent ecosystems. It means evolving from outputs to outcomes, and from pushed to pulled products and services. I will explain all of this in a moment, but to provide context, let me first share the illustration of the Banking Reinvention Quadrant.

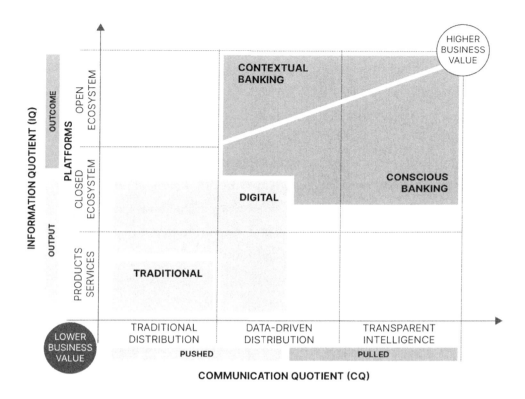

Figure 1: The Banking Reinvention Quadrant
Source: Paolo Sironi, *"Banks and Fintech on Platform Economies: Contextual and Conscious Banking"*,
Wiley (2021)

As you can see, the Banking Reinvention Quadrant is built on two axes:
"Information Quotient" and "Communication Quotient." This reflects
the new reality that the changing role of information and communication
is the real driver of business **transformation**.

The Information Quotient is the "technology" axis, representing the transformation towards **open** ecosystems and platform economies based on open banking, open finance, and Decentralized Finance (DeFi). The Communication Quotient is the "business" axis, representing the intensity of AI use to support the digital transformation of relationships.

Traditionally, information—which shapes the structure of core banking processes—has had a dominant role, permitting financial intermediaries to generate charter value, making them more stable and forward-looking. But the landscape is changing. The role of communication is taking a more central role in determining the industry structure, and its impact may now eclipse that of information.

Communication **supported by AI** becomes the sustainable structure of digital innovation, because it enables banks to re-invent client engagement. As illustrated in the Banking Reinvention Quadrant, the relationship between communication and information leads to **Conscious Banking** and **Contextual Banking**. Both are higher-business value models. What they have in common is the sharing of information through cloud-based, open finance platforms, and the enrichment of client communication with transparent, robust, and explicable artificial intelligence solutions.

Contextual Banking is a deep reinvention of bank engagement models via the invisible embedding of banking and financial offers inside non-banking ecosystems. Contextual Banking is underpinned by a banking-as-a-service architecture that embraces outcome economies at a very high level, leveraging open finance to organize complex ecosystems and create tremendous value. Think of Bank of Baroda in India with its ability to embed known banking services inside what would normally be a non-banking ecosystem of agricultural information. Contextual Banking platforms are information-intensive. They leverage open finance and exponential technologies to eliminate frictions in non-banking ecosystems, embedding invisible services into the user journeys of other industries. They enable banks to own the engagement layer and design, and so orchestrate the customer experience and every engagement.

Conscious Banking is about the transparent transformation of bank business models from transactions to services, centered on "value-based" banking relationships. Banks improve their Information Quotient by creating more open platforms capable of integrating value from external providers, especially non-banking insights that contribute to orchestrating the financial well-being of platform users. They increase their Communications Quotient to support the content and breadth of advisory relationships. Clients are aware they engage in banking relationships, but demand a single point of touch via a digital ecosystem platform which can consolidate finance frameworks across all assets, liabilities and services. Conscious Banking platforms are communication-intensive. They leverage exponential technologies and transparent relationships to unlock value, assisting clients and intermediaries to consciously manage financial lifestyles.

Steps to reinventing banking models

If you look at the examples we started out with—DBS Bank in Singapore, Bank of Baroda, and State Bank of India—each has successfully adapted their business and technology frameworks to achieve higher business value with particular emphasis on the Contextual Banking platform strategy.

Every bank will have its own path to digital transformation, but in my experience, there are three common characteristics among all banks that are vital to successful business model reinvention.

First, reinvention must start at the top. It requires commitment from the CEO and Board. It's not just technology or communication that must change; it is the entire culture of the organization. There must be a top-down commitment to new ways of working; new ways of communicating; new ways of engaging with customers; new ways of incentivizing employees and customers.

Second, a process and model to allow new methodology to be designed and tested before it goes live is required. This means creating a "value engine room" in which all hypotheses for technological, cultural, and organizational changes can be tested. Because digital transformation is both strategic and all-encompassing, services must be rolled out nimbly, and providers must be quick to learn how to adjust them continuously to meet customer needs.

Third, digital transformation and the shift to contextual and conscious banking models cannot happen without an underlying infrastructure. That's where the value of cloud models, platforms, and open systems come into play. With the right infrastructure, banks should be able to connect data from internal and external sources in a secure way. They can leverage continuous feedback loops between their organization, developers, partners, and the rest of their ecosystem in a secure, compliant environment—taking advantage of open standards, microservices, intrinsic security, cloud-native services, and end-to-end resiliency.

Lessons learned

The last years of FinTech innovation have demonstrated the prowess of digital technology, but also highlighted relevant roadblocks to completing digital transformations, generating value for clients, and improving the industry's financial performance.

FinTech besieged banking, but didn't conquer **all** client engagement as many innovators did not understand that mobile technology is— **primarily**—a technology of the demand. It requires users to self-direct themselves: clients must autonomously pull what they need in terms of financial and banking consumption. Instead, most of the revenues that matter in a banking world of high costs of capital, low interest rates, and product commoditization are generated in an offer-driven economy. However integrated by data and insights, products are "pushed" to clients through human relationships, as most clients are incapable of directing themselves—especially in investing and insuring. This gap can be digitally reduced with the hyper-personalized contextualization of financial decision-making inside the user journeys, and the transparent provision of advice that leverages digital technology. Remember the earlier examples of how banks have already embraced transformation? Bank of Baroda's use of specialized non-banking data such as crop conditions and market prices? DBS Bank's car marketplace and travel solution? These examples can inspire innovation and Engagement Banking transformation using Contextual Banking, and Conscious Banking.

The Banking Reinvention Quadrant allows us to systematize our understanding of what is really going on inside the financial intermediation of products and services—and look at the role of information and communication below the surface, to guide bankers and entrepreneurs in positioning an offer-driven economy on a demand-driven technology.

1. "SBI YONO Has A Valuation Of Over $40 Billion, Chairman Rajnish Kumar Says", Bloomberg, September 2020, https://www.bloombergquint.com/business/sbi-yono-has-a-valuation-of-over-dollar40-billion-chairman-rajnish-kumar-says
2. "STOXX Changes Composition of Sector Indices effective June 22nd, 2020" Stoxx, June 13, 2020, https://www.stoxx.com/document/News/2020/June/Index%20Update_STOXX_Component_Changes_Sector_Indices_20200613.pdf
3. IBM Institute of Business Value, "Unlock the Business Value of Hybrid Cloud", originally published July 20, 2021

Key decision points and takeaways

One of the important factors in business model innovation is in changing the relationship between the bank and its customers. It's not only about offering products and services that your customers love; it's also about making them pay for services that must be transparent and can be embedded. That's the ultimate value of evolving to Contextual Banking and Conscious Banking business models.

So, what are the practical steps banking leaders can take today to adopt the principles of the Banking Reinvention Quadrant and begin the journey toward next-generation banking business models? Here are some key decision points and takeaways to help you on your journey:

- **Change the culture from product-centric propositions to human-centric propositions.** This is paramount. It implies a revision of the incentive mechanisms inside the organization. The intermediation with clients in the "outcome economy" is based on transformed mechanics of revenue generation.
- **Embrace the open organization.** An advanced operating model leveraging secured API-based data-sharing inside and outside the organization is the backbone required to transform culture. According to recent research by IBM, the Institute of Business Value, combining end-to-end digital transformation with the open organization is the most important driver to unlock the business value of investments in cloud-based infrastructure.[3]
- **Rethink cyber security as a business enabler.**

Key decision points and takeaways (continued)

Modern innovation on cloud, interfacing open ecosystems, must be based on trusted development and deployment of new services, solutions, and business models. Only a "shift-left" of security operations allows resiliency while intensifying the Information Quotient with the speed required to outdo the competition.

- **Invest in a modern data platform that allows secured links between proprietary and external data sources.** A well thought through data fabric precedes the AI architecture to make AI applications truly transparent, robust, and explicable. This grants speed in the usage of AI to intensify the Communication Quotient.

- **Embrace transparency in all services and solutions.** Transparency is a competitive advantage in a world made of product standardization, lower transactional margins, and digital disintermediation. It allows new business models to unlock hidden value in the banking relationship based on Conscious Banking platforms—platforms supporting holistic advisory relationships remunerated from client fees. The transparent relationship is the product that clients can pay for accessing the platform.

- **Orchestrate new platforms at the intersection with adjacent ecosystems to address the needs of affine communities.** Embedding banking capabilities to eliminate friction in user engagement allows Contextual Banking platforms to unlock new value, permitting them to monetize the entire ecosystems. The trusted and frictionless engagement is the product that clients can pay for accessing the platform.

Chapter 5

Discarding old biases and norms to embrace disruption

Ben Morales, Chief Technology Officer and Operations Officer, Washington State Employees Credit Union

In most facets of our lives, we crave and search for normalcy. It's human nature to seek consistent, predictable patterns to our personal and work lives in order to feel confident, comfortable, and secure. We may not know what's around the corner, but understanding "the rules of the game" helps us to anticipate the impact of disruption.

But guess what? Normalcy isn't all it's cracked up to be.

More and more often, trying to avoid disruption, change, and discomfort forces us back into old, familiar patterns; we fail to understand that avoiding change also means **missing opportunities**. It might make us feel better at home and work when we can continue to do things the way we always have—but clinging to old biases and norms can be not only counter-productive, but also downright dangerous.

As uncomfortable as it may make us feel, we should all **embrace** disruption—especially in our work.

And there aren't many industries in which it's more important to embrace disruption and cast aside old biases and norms than in banking and financial services. Whether it's about how and where we bank, or the new and often-confusing regulatory maze, or the cacophony of marketing messages from new market entrants, disruption abounds.

That's actually OK. Because us transforming our industry, our organizations—or you transforming your own job—can be therapeutic and even liberating. It can help all of us see our customers, employees, and our own missions in new and exciting ways.

I think that's why so many people in so many industries in so many parts of the world are wholeheartedly embracing the once-buzzword-but-now-corporate-mantra of "digital transformation."

Pundits will tell you that digital transformation is about embracing concepts like mobility, cloud computing, blockchain, anything-as-a-service and user experience—and there's a lot of truth there. But digital transformation—and in fact the broader transformation in Engagement Banking in financial services—is really about understanding that the day you fail to get out in front of change is **the day you start promoting your own organizational decline.**

Let me offer you a word of advice: don't.

Our journey to transformation (with a shortcut through disruption pass)

I believe I'm on solid ground here because I can speak of our own credit union's first-hand experiences. We struggled, fought, and thrashed about in the face of industry-wide disruption, even while we continued to enjoy business success. We were aware disruption was happening but not immediately sure of what to do about it. One thing we did know, however, was that sticking with our old ways, old systems, and old approaches would not be acceptable.

Make no mistake: Financial services in general, and credit unions specifically, have had to navigate through a morass of disruption since the early 2010s. New competitors, new technologies, new rules, and especially, new customer demands—all of these represented substantial disruption on their own—and collectively they were like climbing Mount Everest in a snowstorm.

For instance: credit unions were dealing with a new federal regulator, the Consumer Finance Protection Board—and with the added pressure and attention it brought to the industry. There was substantial merger and acquisition activity both among credit unions and between credit unions and banks. Membership skyrocketed even as the number of credit unions dwindled as a byproduct of those mergers.

But as usual the members themselves were the biggest drivers of disruption, and much of that disruption centered on how, when, and where they used technology to make their financial transactions. Requirements such as mobile remote deposit capture, member self-service, and anytime/anywhere mobile banking were no longer negotiable for financial institutions; it was time to step up or step aside.

Like many of my colleagues in the credit union and banking space, I watched the move toward mobility, cloud, and a more seamless user experience, and I knew where we were headed. But this was around 2014, and the need to invest in the underlying technology (and the necessary expertise) was not well understood or readily accepted by many credit unions' executives.

For our organization, the good news was we had made solid investments in online and mobile banking a few years earlier. The bad news was our (then) technology provider for our online and mobile banking platform wasn't keeping up with the inexorable force being exerted by our members. Our then-partner was either unable to deploy the functions we needed—and our members demanded—fast enough, or at all.

We found ourselves playing catch-up with our competitors. Not an enviable spot, to be sure.

And if that wasn't bad enough it was very clear to me, my team, and many of our top executives that this rate of change was only going to **accelerate.** Our members had shown an insatiable appetite for technology to allow them far more freedom in their banking needs, and of course we had to give them not only a superior experience, but also a safe, secure, resilient, and reliable platform to handle more and more functions.

The digital world was exploding before our very eyes, and we weren't just fighting with one arm behind our back—we were using a first-generation platform while our competitors were deploying digital warfare. We were missing out on new requirements such as remote deposit capture and travel alerts, to name just a couple. It was impacting our brand, and we were worried—no, we were scared—that the likely acceleration of member demands would stifle our growth without a new approach to digital banking.

As these and other forces for disruption came together simultaneously, I asked myself and my team: *"Where are we going to change? Why and how?"* Clearly, we needed our banking platform to do more than it was designed to do. It was time for a new platform, which would most likely mean a new partner. Changing a core technology platform as you embark on a strategic journey in an era of massive disruption is never an inviting prospect, but we had no choice. Without a new partner, there would be no new platform. And without a new platform, we could not create competitive differentiation and satisfy our members' current and future needs.

We understood that while we needed to own the Engagement Banking experience for our members, we didn't need—or want—to own the infrastructure and the rest of the plumbing. We needed a partner to allow us to focus on creating an innovative member experience, and for them to provide a next-generation-plus platform that would not only drive more engagement with current members, but also act as a magnet for future, most likely younger, members.

The good news is we were introduced to Backbase. Backbase had already achieved success in the mainstream banking industry but hadn't yet found a flagship customer in the credit union space for its engagement platform. We quickly determined they were not only a strong technology fit, but also an excellent **cultural** fit for our organization.

Most importantly, their experience with banks had prepared them for what happens when organizations cling to old biases and norms in the face of intense, relentless disruption. And we had a checklist of examples: the focus on growth with retail branches. The belief the move to digital would not happen as quickly as it did. The concern about plowing big investments into technologies that went far beyond what we were currently doing. The question of how our in-house team would handle the deployment. The traditionally conservative, risk-averse nature of the financial service industry—which was an especially relevant point, as we still "looked" successful.

What I had learned over my years in the credit union industry is that disruption, while rarely a pleasant experience, often forces organizations to change the way they think and act much faster than would otherwise be the case. The key factor is how far an organization is willing to push itself in enduring the discomforts of disruption.

So, how far would that be in our case?

We were about to find out.

Selling the Board

Transformation can't succeed without great ideas, attentive planning, committed team members, and intense preparation. But there's more. It also can't succeed without the proper funding.

That means getting your C-suite executives and especially your Board, onboard. Nothing perks up a Board member's ears more than the word "transformation" (trust me, I know... I'm a Board member myself). Transformation, whether you're talking about engagement transformation or transforming an entire credit union's mission, can't happen without the enthusiastic support of the Board. Just getting the Board's approval is not enough; the Board must be **all-in on the mission**.

In our case, I realized that selling the board would not be an event; it would be an essential part of a long-term effort marked by information, education, and visioning. I wanted to make sure our Board would not only OK our recommendations, but also co-champion our ideas.

Caution: It's not a small undertaking to recruit your Board for true support. For us, it was a two-year process. We started by building a solid foundation of truths, goals, and challenges everyone could agree with, and that I encouraged Board members to contribute to. We had to raise awareness that staying the course was not just risky, but reckless—and to do so in a way that conveyed a sober analysis of the situation, rather than an alarmist ploy designed to fatten our operating budget.

Disruption and disintermediation were powerful and growing forces of change in our industry, and we spent a lot of time educating our Board on:

A. What was happening.

B. Why it was happening.

C. How those changes would impact our credit union.

I had a lot of data, especially from third parties, and a lot of anecdotes from speaking with members and our employees who dealt with those customers on the front lines. That allowed us to have fact-based, honest, and pragmatic conversations with management and the Board about what could happen if we did not understand and embrace the reality of disruption.

Without laying that foundation, we would not have been able to sell the idea of a high-performance engagement platform, considering the fact our under-performing legacy digital platform **was** still generating business for us. We had to show what we were missing out on, and what we **would** miss out on, without modernization.

To motivate our Board to make that investment and stand behind our efforts, we needed to create a compelling vision of the organization—a sort of "state of the (credit) union" moment.

In particular, we set out to show the Board that the millennials or Gen Z-ers who weren't yet our members—but whom we needed to bring into the fold—could be won over by a state-of-the-art engagement platform whose functionality mirrored how, when, and where those potential members preferred (or should I say demanded?) to make their financial transactions. Those younger members we already had were unsparing in telling us about their frustrations with our legacy platform's functionality limitations—thank goodness they didn't hold back.

Another thing we did that helped was paint a vivid picture of our points of differentiation and why those mattered. We knew it wasn't enough to match what was already in the market; even an historically successful credit union like ours wouldn't achieve goals of transformation in a sea of sameness. Once again, our recommendations on functionality, presentation, user experience, and key performance indicators had to be fact-based—but we also had to learn how to tell poignant stories rooted in the words and experiences of our members.

Finally, we had to be willing to stick our necks out there, and explain how our organization might have to endure, or even promote, workforce disruption. How maybe we'd need to reorganize to put the right people in the right places under the new plan. How maybe some people would need to be promoted, and others might not have the right skills to thrive in the new environment. We have always prided ourselves on being a great organization to work for, so we needed a plan to make everyone successful; even those who might want to cling to old biases and norms in an era of disruption.

What we accomplished and learned

One smart step we took (and which helped get the Board's buy-in) was deciding against an all-or-nothing mentality of investment. Boiling the ocean is rarely a smart operational strategy, and it would have been imprudent to ask the Board to commit to very large upfront expenditures without some display of progress before making additional investments.

Our incremental-investment strategy paid off. We made targeted investments in improving key functionality areas we had prioritized early on, and by the time we got to the core banking system, we'd already implemented a lot of the digital capabilities our current and potential members told us they wanted. It probably took a good 18 months to build awareness and urgency with our Board, our executive team, and our business stakeholders. That last group—the different business units—will be really important to your process because any part of your credit union with a digital product has to connect through your platform. If you add functionality, but negatively impact performance in their core area, someone is going to be very unhappy—and you don't need bad internal publicity in the early stages of your implementation.
What have we accomplished? Plenty.

Our number of products accessed per member household through digital channels is way up, and so is our revenue. We've significantly reduced in-person or call-based service requests by putting a premium on member self-service. And our user experience ratings are just as high as they were when delivering member service was less complex than it is today; probably even higher in many instances. We know that because our Net Promoter score tells us that our members' digital experiences are highly positive. I won't kid you; it wasn't always a walk in the park.

Engagement Banking transformation is easy to say but much harder to achieve—especially when you are continually confronted with old patterns of usage and legacy preferences among members and employees. We often had to confront and overcome inertia too, even in the operations group. We didn't catch how pervasive that was for about six-to-nine months; and then spent more time on re-inventing processes, re-educating teams, and re-emphasizing goals and anticipated benefits. We also had to constantly remind everyone our focus had to be on the primary source of all the disruption we were facing and were ever likely to face: the members.

We learned how important it is to develop the right skills inside our organization to complement the capabilities and expertise of our technology partner. We needed people who could help us break down the walls created by organizational inertia, and help move programs along faster to operationalize our engagement platforms more effectively. Remember, the faster you can operationalize your strategies and investments, the faster you can show results. That's not only good for your top and bottom lines, but also essential in helping you retain and expand support inside your organization. Lots of small wins—like lots of small software releases—really add up fast.

Transforming transformation

That last point is something very important for banks, credit unions, and all financial institutions to remember when trying to use an engagement platform mentality to drive customer engagement. It's best to strive for relatively small, frequent, and iterative releases of new functionality, rather than pursuing the big-bang approach.

If this sounds remarkably like the DevOps mentality of software development, there's a good reason—the DevOps mentality works. For those of you not steeped in software development knowledge, here's a quick primer.

For many decades, banks have relied on large, expensive, and monolithic mainframe computers for transactional systems (many still do to this day, for a variety of applications). In that environment, software development was a slow process; an arduous slog that focused on major software overhauls over long periods of time: the "Waterfall" method. That method has been overhauled in the past decade and largely replaced by the DevOps mentality of "Agile" software development, marked by many and **frequent** releases of small improvements which add up over time and deliver substantial value—even with small releases.

That was the model we used at the credit union to drive our Engagement Banking transformation through our new engagement platform: faster releases, more frequent updates and upgrades, new revenue sources, and new opportunities for member engagement.

Another thing we learned, that should seem obvious but is often overlooked, is to **listen to your members.** And don't just ask them—**listen** really, really close. If you ask your members, they will tell you. But be forewarned: If you ask them what they want you to do, they will actually expect you to do it. If you don't follow through and give them what they need and want, you are going to be in deep trouble.

Let me share a few short tips based on our experience:

- Start with an understanding among management and Board that there is either a problem or an opportunity that must be addressed. Without acknowledging that, it's difficult to get your executives to act and become clarions for change.
- Learn how to become a story-teller. And if you or others on your team aren't good at that skill (it isn't easy, trust me), invest in someone who is. It helps a lot in getting your stakeholders to envision what you're doing and why. When you talk to the Board, you don't want head-nodding; you want animated discussion and people rising up out of their seats.
- Rely on facts and data, although be careful not to overwhelm people with arcane data points. Select a few powerful, poignant, and relevant facts and data, and lean into them—and keep the focus on outcomes.

Also: keep in mind that disruption, even when properly acknowledged, anticipated, and planned for is going to be unsettling for your organization and your people. The key is to understand it and not be paralyzed by fear of it. The best way to do that is to over-emphasize communication, discussion, and honest conversation; especially in the early phase of your Engagement Banking transformation project.

Lastly, be sure to balance your own confidence and resolve with a dash of humility. I didn't know it all—and I still don't—but I understood that acknowledging where and when to rely on others, both inside and outside our organization, was key to our success.

I hope you will find the journey as exciting as I did.

Chapter 6

Defining the KPIs for Engagement Banking transformation success

Mayur Vichare, Head of Value Consulting, Backbase

Only 16% of banks that have embarked upon an Engagement Banking transformation **know whether it was actually successful.**[1]

Why?

Well, I've seen the Engagement Banking transformation of several banks and read about the journey of several more—and from my experience the answer is very simple.

It's because only 16% of banks **define success metrics at the start of their Engagement Banking transformation and continue to track those metrics throughout it.**

So, only those banks can know if they've successfully transformed.

I've worked with change leaders, and successful banks that employed the right leadership, team, and strategies to identify their goals and metrics—and not just to create their initial business case, but also to ensure they were making the right impact as they went along.

In this chapter I'll share my learnings with you. I'll show you powerful ways to secure executive sign-off, and enable you to ensure you're set up to measure and demonstrate success to your executive team throughout your bank's transformation.

The catalyst of change

Changing the course of a bank from traditional methods of client engagement and employee incentivization to true Engagement Banking may seem like an impossible task.

There are many reasons why banks are slow to change—from siloed business units, to outdated or incomplete data repositories, to executive reluctance. The start point for change is often the business case.

First, it's the enabler to gain alignment across the bank. Second, it provides a framework for executives to sign off the investment. Third—and most importantly—a correctly created business case relates directly to the success of any Engagement Banking transformation—by providing the measures of success to track improvements driven through it.

Let's start by talking about how change is sparked.

The biggest obstacles for Engagement Banking transformation I've seen are a lack of internal transparency and a lack of honesty. I've seen executives just not listening to their people working on the ground. I've witnessed CEOs expecting an independent consultant to create a transformation strategy without even talking to the executive team to understand what's happening currently. Internal transparency and honesty are critical. They're vital to break down business silos and get your teams working together.

For instance: we worked with the CIO for a bank in Asia. His main goal was to gain alignment across all heads of business. The largest obstacle to achieving his goal was the lack of customer data transparency—especially because one specific business unit was not prepared to share customer data at all. This meant if a customer bought a loan, the deposit product unit couldn't even see that customer. We were brought in to bring the department heads together to create the ideal customer journey, irrespective of department, which enabled them to put a business case together for Engagement Banking.

And that's often why executives bring in someone from the outside—to hold up a mirror. Sometimes that's what it takes for a CEO to see the need for change. It doesn't matter how much their people have already tried to shake the tree.

I personally think changing a bank is a little easier if there is a revolutionary person—a "Catalyst for change"—inside that bank who can help bring it about.

Someone who can challenge the status quo. Someone who can bring the CEO and Directors on board with the vision of change by force of personality. Someone who knows how to create a compelling event rather than just saying *"Everything is wrong."* Perhaps, for instance, by showing benchmarking—comparing the bank not just to peers but also to new players who are eating into their business. Remember, typically, traditional bank executives regard interest income, fees, and commissions as most important—not customer loyalty and engagement.

This may mean the Catalyst needs to create a mindset shift among the executives.

It's also important to note what the Catalyst **cannot** be.

To function effectively as a change leader, they can't be the acting head of a business unit—at least, not in the traditional sense. Bank business units traditionally work in a highly siloed fashion—staff only focus on the success of their own products (like loans, deposit products, or real estate). This is contrary to the customer-centric model which focuses on the success and engagement of the customer across multiple channels and products. To be successful, the Catalyst must be able to set aside the narrow focus of a single product and instead be able to think and act across multiple business units.

This is one reason many banks I've seen have created a distinct office of the CDO (chief digital officer), or sometimes a chief experience officer—headed by a thought leader tasked with charting the enterprise's digital future. This "change leader" position would be ideal for the Catalyst, but if the bank isn't yet willing to formally create this role a temporary but distinct team should be created—and led—by someone with appropriate seniority, skill, and vision. Of course, this leader must be able to lead an agile transformation. Once transformation starts, they'll need to demonstrate value starting with an MVP while simultaneously moving on a long-term strategy to transform—enabling the bank to catch up with, and overtake, the competition.

Banks often justify digital change efforts based on features or technology used by their competitors (which I will discuss further, below) without having a clear idea about why the feature is necessary or how it fits in with a business or customer strategy. But in my experience, successful Catalysts for engagement transformation instinctively understand and sense the opportunities of emerging digital technologies and digitally enabled business models. A Catalyst will be able to discern and describe what is relevant and what is not—both for the long-term success of their bank and for the satisfaction and engagement of its customers. They can translate customer-centric success metrics—things like loyalty, engagement, retention, and effort—into business success metrics.

The change leader and their team will need to build and maintain relationships with vendors, including startups, that may be new or even foreign to the bank. Banks have a strong "build it ourselves" culture which can stand in the way of agility and innovation. Successful change leaders understand the startup culture and how to enable change—which often means bringing it in from the outside via partnerships or vendors. Similarly, successful change leaders often have or create relationships with academic partners who are pitching change within the banking world.

All of this focus on change and transformation makes it difficult to name a Catalyst, a change leader, from within a bank. It may be best to consider hiring from the outside to ensure a fresh perspective—especially if the new leader has the experience and connections you need. Alternatively, you could have a temporary team led by a consultant—but for the longer term, there needs to be an internal leader.

The teams for change

I can't stress this enough: your Catalyst must be able to function outside of your normal business silos. They need to be able to maintain their independence to correctly assess how the business case is being built; without any preference, or loyalty to current business practices, results, data, and policies.

The Catalyst will then need to create two teams: the team for transformation, and the development team.

The team for transformation

They should be drawn from a variety of internal teams and roles depending on the transformation—such as branch, call center, back office, web and mobile, and marketing teams. You can't just focus on the web and mobile team, or you'll end up with beautiful web pages or mobile apps that have customers wasting 20 days to do something that should only take a few hours.

Branch, call center, and back-office staff bring important insights into how things work at a bank, and working together they can think holistically about how the customer experience should work across the business units. Marketing teams—especially brand, design, and communications—typically have valuable familiarity with customer experience. They can help to ensure that branding and style are consistent while incorporating scalable and flexible design models. Marketing teams also bring connections with external vendors who can be powerful partners in both the near- and long-term. This business team will be involved throughout the design, development, testing, and deployment phases of the MVP and overall transformation. But, bottom line: they all need to be stakeholders in the investment and are key to building the business case.

The development team

This team will depend on the bank's existing technology. Can the MVP and the ultimate transformation be developed and maintained on existing frameworks? Remember your solution needs to be flexible, agile, and scalable—there will be lots of testing, experimentation, and iterations. If the internal frameworks don't work, you should bring in an outside solution, and then consider if you can use an internal development team or if you need to bring in a consultant. All of this is critical to think through as you build the business case because it all adds to the budget you request, your planning, and success criteria.

There are two additional roles I recommend for the team that are probably new for the bank.

First, there should be a business consultant and analyst who will be responsible for translating data into metrics that measure success of the MVP and transformation to demonstrate clear business value. The core business team members understand how their businesses work, but they aren't IT people—they will need a business consultant and analysts to tease the data out of the bank systems and translate it into metrics that measure the customer journey. Second, there needs to be a product owner: someone who understands Agile development and has an eye on the goals from a product development perspective; someone who can communicate effectively to help other teams work in an agile way.

First steps toward change

The immediate focus should be on establishing a connection between customer metrics and business goals.

As a catalyst, you can look at three key pillars - Customer Acquisition, Customer Servicing and Retention, and Digital Operating model.

> **Customer acquisition:** Focuses on acquiring customers at a faster pace with the lowest cost. Digital plays a big role here. Tracking how many accounts are opened through digital channels is a key metric in understanding brand, product, technology, and pricing positioning in the market.

> **Customer servicing and retention:** Focuses on how to provide exceptional service at the lowest cost while retaining the customers. Customer loyalty is key and a subset of customer servicing. The greater the loyalty, the more products held by the customer. Customer loyalty is often measured by NPS—however, the NPS is measured twice a year. NPS should be measured at a journey level across channels. A better digital customer self-service directly corresponds to loyalty in banking and financial services today— especially since the pandemic. Better adoption of digital services also directly leads to cost savings.

Digital operating model: This is all about how agile you are and the technology that supports your organization. Examples of key metrics could be: time taken to release new features, or time taken to make changes to current digital offerings.

Let's take the example of customer acquisition. This may be the first time these metrics are being measured, so you may need to expend some effort to get a "before" value:

Customers come to your website to research and learn about a certain bank product. They come with the intent to learn, engage, and maybe buy. Some fraction of those who arrive at the bank's website find the product page and click through. A fraction of those customers starts the process to purchase the product. A fraction of those end up completing the process. This leakage at each step can happen for a variety of reasons. But often even the leakage itself isn't being measured by the bank— and yet, simply reducing the loss (from initial engagement through to purchase) has obvious revenue potential that anyone in the bank can understand.

You can imagine the opening statement from the Catalyst to the CEO:

"I've been looking at how many potential customers we lose between when they show up at our website and when they sign up for a new account. In our space it's typically 27%. But for us it's over 45%. We should change that. It will generate more revenue and make us more profitable."

With a focus on customer acquisition, your team will start with an assessment of the current state. How do you acquire customers now? What are examples of the best-in-market methods? What are the ways you can improve this customer journey? Once you've answered those questions, you'll have a high-level idea of what you want to achieve and you can think about possible solutions.

This would be a good time to talk to the CIO (chief information officer) to see if you can make this work within the framework you have today. You might even try a quick effort on your existing framework—but it's critical that you have a modular, scalable, agile platform to use for your testing. For example, clients in different countries may need different solutions for a particular customer journey, so your platform needs to be flexible and agile to allow you to quickly address specific problems—or test alternative solutions—faster. If you simply don't have the internal capability, you will have to go outside and get help from a third party. But be sure they have the flexibility and capability you'll need.

This may be an appropriate time to think about the bank's longer-term goals for conversion to either a transformed business model or a Neobank model, based on how the bank itself functions and its current technological capabilities.

Early on—ideally as you create the business case—recruit end consumers in different constituencies and in different walks of life for surveys, mock-ups, interviews, and testing throughout the development process. This will be your customer advisory panel. Remember your goals, and ask them about their decisions and thoughts during the acquisition process. What reasons do they have for coming to the bank in the first place? What are the money or life problems they hope to resolve? What drives them forward or drives them away? Maybe they don't understand something that you think is obvious, or they miss something you think is clear. You need to understand the current ("as-is") state and existing friction from the customer's perspective to be able to achieve the customer journey end state. Ask, probe, experiment, and see what works and what doesn't for these customers.

These insights are critical to demonstrate what the customer has to go through now, and then show the vision of what you will create, and the value it will bring to the business. Keep in mind that you are in the business case stage. Metrics are critical to establish at this stage and continue into transformation as you start implementation. Remember, your transformation is a journey. How you measure success and show progress to the Board and the rest of your business is critical to ensure they stay on the journey with you.

Let's focus on how you can define those metrics now.

Measuring success

Three years after I worked with one bank to implement a digital solution, I went back and asked what they had achieved in terms of revenue and cost. *"We didn't track that,"* they answered. Too often banks think the KPI is that they developed a digital solution.

With your business case, you will be focused on a small number of key metrics to report success to the bank's executive suite—things like adoption rate (or leakage) and cost to serve (e.g., via call center call rates). The core business team may want to start to track additional metrics to measure—especially once you start to build the MVP. For instance:

- **Time to acquire a product or service.** How long does it take a customer to sign up or purchase?
- **Wait time to solve.** How long does it take to resolve an issue reported by the customer?
- **Customer engagement.** How likely is the customer to want additional services or products?
- **Customer effort.** How difficult is it for the customer to get or find what they need? This is a subjective measure from the customer's perspective—often discovered via surveys.
- **Customer satisfaction.** Were they able to get the help they needed? Would they recommend the bank or service to someone else? Measure this immediately after the customer experience, not months later.
- **Cost to build.** How much did it cost to build a feature or a service?

- **Time to resolve.** How long does it take to resolve internal change requests? Bugs?
- **Innovation.** How many new things did we launch in a given time period?
- **Scalability, efficiency, time to market.** All are aspects of cost reduction.

Many of these will be important in the bank's longer-term transformation to Engagement Banking, so start to measure them right away and work towards creating a metric-driven culture. The success of the bank—and the internal reward system—needs to be based on these kinds of metrics.

At a top level, there are really three key metrics that you will report to the CEO and the Board:

1. **Profit per customer.** New customer acquisition is extremely difficult, so banks should focus on how to get the most out of the customers they have already acquired, either by fixing the basics or introducing new banking and/or non-banking services.
2. **Profit per employee.** Banking has become a commodity. The distribution model has to focus on providing services with stripped down branches and ATMs, with more focus on enabling employees with tools to provide best services at the lowest cost. Making this metric extremely important, too.
3. **Returns on digital investments.** CEOs should keep a clear track of these. More often than not, major investments are

made in technology without a clear tracking of their returns.

It's critical that you get a "before" state for as many of the metrics you will track as possible, even if you have to estimate it. Sometimes the most difficult part is simply getting the data out of a bank's systems. During a six-to-eight week consulting engagement, at least half my time is spent trying to acquire the data. It can be both an IT and a bureaucracy problem because there are so many disparate channels with their own databases and it's difficult to extract the data.

For example, I worked with a client to try to understand why customers were reaching out to the bank via more expensive channels—like the call center—when they had the bank's mobile app or access via the web. The call center data was so poorly maintained and designed, the bank couldn't get any insights from it. If you find yourself in a similar situation, figure out how to track calls for some reasonable period (say 15-30 days) and extrapolate it to set an appropriate baseline.

It may be hard to get the initial state, but it's even more critical to establish systems and processes to gather and monitor the data going forward, so be sure that's part of the plan (and the budget!).

"Loyalty" may be a long-term goal for the bank, but one difficult to demonstrate through the strategy development. Still, there are ways to probe your test customers to see if the changes you're making might lead them to want to do more with your bank—which is a form of loyalty.

When your bank becomes one people love, you can bring in outside services you don't own, but can orchestrate—giving more value to your customers, and ultimately receiving more revenue.

Challenges

The business case can also help you stay ahead of challenges once you start the transformation. Creating the business case to help address these up front will help you have a smoother implementation process and take into account cost modelling:

> **Data:** It can be extremely difficult to get data from existing bank systems. Metrics and a metric-driven culture are critical to the success of Engagement Banking, so you need to solve the data issue—both to measure the "as-is" state of the bank and the success or failure of your experimentation. You may need entirely new data systems. Don't forget the business analysts and data architects.

> **IT:** Systems and frameworks need to be agile, scalable, and flexible. You need to be able to rapidly test and iterate, release new products and update existing ones, and adapt to different customer demographics and needs. Existing IT systems may not be up to the task, so you may need to bring in third party systems and platforms to help. At the same time, banks have a strong "build it yourself" culture that can stand in the way of using best-of-breed solutions, so there may be some cultural challenges as well as technological ones.

Design: Homegrown solutions are often difficult to maintain or change because of fundamental design considerations–both the platform and the interface need to have modularity, scalability, and flexibility designed in. Too often technical debt has grown on top of short-sighted design decisions and the rework cost for IT is too high, so technical debt grows out of control.

Similarly, design considerations around the user interface impact web and app designers–if the widgets or screens aren't built on top of flexible and scalable standards, designers are forced to do a lot of rework. If the bank brings in systems built on standards, or ones that enable the bank to establish and maintain standards, there's less rework and less debt; and designers and developers can spend more time experimenting and adding new features.

Transparency: Traditional bank models rely on often hidden fees and commissions, and customers hate that. In the engagement model, costs are made clear to the customer. This is a difficult change for traditional banks, but demonstrating that customer value clearly maps to business value will sell the story.

Internal insecurity: Many staff members will be worried about losing their jobs as the bank transitions. Business unit executives will be worried about losing turf or losing control of "their" portion of the business. Instead, bank leaders must create a comfort zone for the existing staff. The message must be: *"We are changing for the future. If there are redundancies as we start to break down silo walls, we will identify* *talent gaps and educate staff to fill those gaps so that existing skills are still used to our advantage."* Staff issues will be amended with talent from outside that bring experience and skills that can be shared, so everyone can be invested in the customer journey. Remember the "profit per employee" metric, above. Staff need to understand they will be given the tools to solve problems for their customers, and rewarded for doing it. Ultimately, the change to Engagement Banking is not just for the good of the customers–it's for the good of the staff, too.

Conclusion

Building the business case for Engagement Banking can be the spark for change that engages teams across your bank. The two key tasks requiring the most diligence are:

- Careful selection of the right Catalyst to lead the change.
- Identifying the success metrics within your business case—and tracking them throughout the transformation to demonstrate your success to executives and your Board—and celebrating that with your team.

Now you know the key ingredients, you'll be able to correctly create a business case for Engagement Banking. One that can align your business, gain Board agreement, put your customer at the heart of your bank, and enable you to drive transformation—and measure its success from start to finish.

Remember: **your business case creates the foundation for your bank's transformation.**

1. "Welcome to the Digital Factory: The answer to how to scale your digital transformation", Mckinsey.com, May 14, 2020, https://www.mckinsey.com/business-functions/mckinsey-digital/our-insights/welcome-to-the-digital-factory-the-answer-to-how-to-scale-your-digital-transformation

Executive Engagement Banking questions

These are some of the questions you or your bank's executives may want to ask the Catalyst (your internal advocate or consultant for the Engagement Banking transformation):

"I've seen our competition implement feature XYZ. How can we get that?" This is exactly the kind of question they shouldn't ask. Sometimes banks look across the street to their competitors to guide their tactical decisions. They think they need to match their competition feature-for-feature to be able to win clients, but this is a very short-sighted way to look at the customer and what they want and expect. Executives who think this way expect these new features will somehow yield more customers and share-of-wallet and earn more revenues in the traditional fees-and-commissions model. But really they are just temporary, cosmetic solutions that don't solve underlying customer dissatisfaction. Instead, they should be asking: *"How do we solve our retention problem?"* or *"What do our customers need?"*

Executive Engagement Banking questions (continued)

"How does this help my business? What's the ROI?" This is the crux of what matters to bank executives—and an opportunity for the Catalyst to explain how Engagement Banking translates into new revenue models, long-term revenue from loyal customers, and growth into new markets and customers.

"How do I track this? How do I measure success?" These are very forward-looking questions given how rarely traditional banks measure customer-related metrics and tie them to revenue and cost. This is a chance to change the culture to be more metric-driven.

"How can we be bolder?" Often banks are too cautious—they don't think beyond the next single step. How can we innovate? How do we gain market share? How do we differentiate?

"How do we keep current customers happy?" and **"Why are our competitor's customers not with us, and how do we get them?"** This is a chance to think beyond the bank, to think about creating a differentiation so even non-consumers of banking services (who are instead going to FinTechs or may not even be investing anywhere) become interested in your bank. This is the promise of Engagement Banking.

Chapter 7

Five crucial decisions: how to successfully start your Engagement Banking transformation

Heidi Custers, Digital Transformation Director, Backbase

I'm one of the fortunate few people who absolutely love their job. How could I not?

I get to work with some of the world's most innovative banking executives—people who are passionate about their customers. I get to engage with them, coach them, and lead them through their banks' transformations. I get to witness their personal fulfillment as their customers express how much they now love their bank; and in turn I get to hear about the results their innovation and leadership bring.

Engagement Banking transformations are not simple though, and I wouldn't want to lead anyone into a misguided perception that they are. We know there is a need to change. Leadership surveys show that over 80% of the world's biggest banks' leaders believe their banks need to transform.[1] And yet, of all Engagement Banking transformations begun, more than 70% have ended in failure.[2] The reason for those failures has a lot to do with how those banks **began** their transformations.

How a bank starts its transformation journey is pivotal. It's the period filled with the most promise—and the most peril—as its transformation team realizes they are about to make a big leap into the unknown.

Most banks' Boards have never been through as broad-reaching a transformation as an Engagement Banking transformation will be; it's difficult for them to advise executives and ask the right questions. Digital leaders are unlikely to be quite prepared for the tremendous pressure that will suddenly fall onto them to make the right decisions to start a transformation and then lead their banks forward through it. Often, banks think teams can deliver transformation at the same time as doing their day job. It's easy to see why so many transformations have ended in failure.

Engagement Banking pioneers have had to find their own paths—without the support of being able to learn from others, or books about the process; without even having a chance to spend ten minutes with someone who's already experienced the journey. It's also very hard to learn from others; it's hard to find the "hows" and "learnings" from those who have successfully led, or been a part of, a transformation.

That's why we've created this book. And why I'm writing this chapter.

To give you the blueprint to start your Engagement Banking transformation successfully and ensure you can showcase the results throughout your journey. To highlight the blind spots you'll be unaware of, so they don't derail your achievements.

In the first 90 days of your journey, you will need to make five crucial decisions to form the bedrock for your Engagement Banking transformation. With that foundation, you can move forward as an agile organization and adapt to whatever comes along. Without it, your chances of success are remote.

In this chapter I will outline those five key decisions and give you the actionable insights to help you identify the choices that most closely align with your bank's DNA. I will also highlight blind spots that could cause you to fail, and show you how to deal with them and stay focused and successful throughout your journey.

Decision one: the Leader

The first choice is always the hardest: who will lead the Engagement Banking transformation? Initially it's often thought to be the Catalyst for change—the one whose evangelism brought the bank together to create the business case; the one who gained executive approval; the one who started everyone on the journey. Often, they **want** to be the one to drive that bank through the execution. But unfortunately, the skills and evangelism needed to drive a bank to business case approval are quite different to the skills needed to bring about its transformation.

To successfully lead through execution, your Leader must be incredibly resilient and a good evangelist—but most importantly a very good translator. They will need to liaise between your Board, your executive committee, and the rest of your organization. They will need to speak the various languages of its different parts, and be able to translate between them to ensure they are unified in what your bank is trying to create. It's a polarizing journey on which the new and old will often be at loggerheads. Your Engagement Banking transformation Leader must be an expert at leading execution, but also a diplomat.

Deloitte calls this Leader the Chief Digital Officer, and describes a persona that is part diplomat, part program manager, and part strategic executive.[3] From my experience, there are two fundamentals of the role which must be understood:

- **It is a full-time, dedicated job:** If your Leader thinks they can lead the transformation execution and "double-hat" with their current job as CMO, CFO, or other CXO, well, that's a hardline **no**. They have to be dedicated to this transformation, because it will take their dedication to lead and ensure they get it right.
- **It is an executive-level position:** This is not a special-projects job. It's an executive role, with an executive mandate, reporting straight to the CEO. This person needs to interface across the entire executive committee and across the entire organization. They need to lead change from the top, across and down throughout the organization.

Without both of those fundamentals being fulfilled, your transformation will be relegated to a project or a program. It will be sidelined, and probably never reach full success. If your Board has agreed to the significant investment to create an engaged bank, then so must you invest in your Leader.

So, should your Leader be an experienced bank insider, or should you bring in an outsider with experience of leading a digital transformation? That depends on your bank's culture.

Your Leader's task will be to **enable**, but it will be up to the rest of your organization to **execute**. An external person will bring fresh energy, an outside perspective, and the experience of having led a digital transformation. For them to succeed, it will be absolutely critical that your bank's culture both supports them and actually executes on the vision. One of the most amazing digital Leaders I worked with was a CFO—in my experience, a Leader can come from anywhere within an organization.

However, this kind of tight, supportive culture is not often seen in very big banks. If your organization's executive committees have their own silos or complex politics, your transformation Leader must be someone your executives know they can trust—an insider. For an internally-sourced leader to succeed, they will often need to work with an external consultant to bring in that outside expertise, transformation experience, and perspective. Alternatively, you might appoint two co-leaders—one from inside and one hired from outside—to act almost as mirror images—in which case a supporting task force may be less critical. I have seen this work before, when both individuals were very mature, secure in their role, and not interested in empire-building.

Your Engagement Banking transformation will be an enormous mind-shift for your executives and everyone else in your organization. MIT Sloan's *The New Elements of Digital Transformation* explains the need to ensure your entire organization—down to procurement, legal, risk, and HR—are aligned and actively supporting the process. MIT Sloan structures their framework as a hierarchy, but I prefer to think of it as a wheel, where all the other elements support, and are supported by, the hub at the center. The employee experience is at the hub of the wheel, right next to the customer—not at the spoke or the rim. Whether you prioritize your customer and/or your employees will be very much driven by the culture of your bank. After that, technology wraps around the hub and enables all of the spokes: your business model, your operations, and your data-driven decision-making to be delivered through the engagement you're crafting.[4]

As the change touches everyone's jobs, all your leaders' KPIs must be changed. In your first 90 days of transformation, your executive committee will need to sit down and take the success measures defined within the business case process and start divvying them up inside the executive committee, ultimately assigning measurements of success to everyone.

Your Leader must take control and responsibility for making sure this massive change is successful across your entire organization.

Your choice of Leader is critical.

Decision two: task force-led vs. CXO-led transition

Once you've got an Engagement Banking transformation Leader in place, it'll be time to decide how to structure your implementation. You probably gave this a lot of thought when developing your business case, so you're likely not starting with a blank slate; but the first 90 days will be the time to make the decision. Are you going to have every CXO lead their own stream (for example, will the CMO be responsible for the customer experience delivered by the platform and success metrics reporting, supported by your chief digital officer), or are you going to take all of the initial measurements and actions and centralize them into a task force?

This is decision two.

As you consider it, look at the culture and motivation of your executive committee to guide you on whether you should choose to give the transformation mandate to your task force or the CXO. If your executive committee is fractured or their plates seem too full fighting operational fires, then a task force needs to lead the transformation and transition the mandate to the executive committee over time.

Regardless of your decision, there's still a place for a task force. It just depends on how big it is and what its implementation mandate is. You may call it the 'transformation office' or the 'value office'—the actual name isn't relevant, as long as it's authentic to the DNA of your company. But there are a few key principles the task force must adopt:

- **It's not a project management office.** The task force is not solely responsible for executing any of the projects in the digital portfolio or roadmap. It enables them. It defines strategy and performs maturity assessments, much like a mini consulting firm. You may already have a project management office or project management capability embedded in your departments. The task force is not replacing those.

- **It's not going to magically change the entire organization on its own.** By its very nature, the task force is temporary. It's done its job when it no longer has a purpose—when the transformation has started to infuse into the organization and it becomes less and less relevant. It's actually working to put itself out of a job.
- **It's staffed with full-time, dedicated personnel.** It's important that the task force doesn't share its responsibilities with another department. Change is hard. The task force needs the opportunity to focus 100% on transition.

Your task force **will** be responsible for sparking change and driving its momentum, but **not** for scaling it to sustainable levels at which it will become "things we do." That's when your departments—or, in ING's case, "tribes," because ING no longer has a traditional banking departmental structure since embarking on an agile transformation—actually take over and start operationalizing the change. That's definitely the next step.

At the start, be as centralized as possible. You will need to identify champions in each of the departments. They don't have to be full-time—they may only spend 20-30% of their time on this effort while they work within their own departments. Nonetheless, they must interface regularly and frequently with the task force. That will help, in the beginning, to keep the cultural shift as smooth as possible—because regardless of how much you try to retain your bank's DNA, you **are** going to shift the culture. It's called transformation for a reason. Even if it's incremental and organic, your bank's culture will change.

In my experience, successful task forces use an Agile methodology. They are principle-led and not process-led. I am passionate about using principles in digital transformation because they allow for flexibility. This means you must populate your task force with people who have a broad range of skills, who think creatively, and who can work across a few disciplines. Then, arm them with a set of principles, give them the freedom to get their job done, and let them know how they'll be measured. Giving them strict processes puts them in the same box as the rest of your bank, which, if it was able to transform on its own, wouldn't need a Leader or a task force.

Remember that your task force is like an internal consulting firm—their job is to interface and educate. They will embed themselves in the business to understand where the problems are, help the departments identify their priorities, pull them into a common framework that everybody can understand, figure out where all the gaps are, and then figure out how to get the momentum started to get things moving.

Use a workshop environment to help develop your own principles. I've done this with my banking customers as an external consultant. You might consider principles like these:

- Make sure that whatever we do, we reduce friction.
- We are going to be capital-light and convert CAPEX to OPEX.
- Let's make sure everything we do has interoperability and ease of integration.

Whatever your principles are, they must be true to the DNA of your bank. If your bank is 190 years old, slow and deliberate, yet one of the task force principles is that absolutely everything they do should be agile and rapid, it's going to be an uphill battle to make that a success measurement for the task force. You must carefully consider all of the implications of each principle, take time to define them, and understand how they impact the task force as well as the rest of your bank. If you understand the implications upfront and stress-test the heck out of them, you'll probably find that you will have principles that are more authentic to your bank's DNA—rather than truisms or values that get stuck on a Post-it no one ever looks at in a room with lots of bean bags.

Decision three: gradual organic change vs. sudden operating model shift

The next key decision: Will your shift be gradual and organic, or sudden and substantial? Your bank's culture and DNA will guide you on which is the better choice—but also, consider the markets in which you operate. In the US, companies like Amazon and Facebook are endangering the banking industry—and in emerging markets like Africa, there's so much transformation and convergence in financial services that there are massive threats coming from sectors such as telecommunications. Market threats like these mean there's considerable impetus to make a "big bang" transformation, requiring a centralized option to allow you to move quickly—because you have to. Alternatively, if you're at a bank where it's more important to transition slowly and incrementally, and your market isn't nipping at your heels, you might give each CXO new KPIs and success measures, and slowly, organically transform the way you do things.

Your bank's culture will really drive this decision.

The bigger banks I've worked with have all tended to go with the more organic approach, and they've seen a little bit more success because they are so big—it takes a big ship a very long time to change direction. That said, there is one notable exception: ING. The ING agile transformation is arguably the most famous digital banking case study in the world.[5] They took an incredibly bold move across their global operations, shifting their entire operating model to agile and digital. It was very difficult, and likely is still very painful for them, but it's certainly a success story of transformation at scale. If you're bold enough to go big bang, it can work—but expect it to take considerably more money than was approved in your business case. If your market demands a big bang change, it may be your only option. However, the vast majority choose to go a little more incrementally.

Whichever option you choose, make your decision early. That way you can spot where you might need to change your thinking and adapt. Maybe you'll be expecting difficulties with getting risk and legal on board—but it'll actually be HR that proves most difficult. That may force you to rethink your people processes. Having more central coordination at the beginning will allow you to spot issues and just shift the strategy a little bit as you need to.

Regardless of whether you decide to take an organic or sudden change, your task force must be the ones to push your organization. It will be uncomfortable. There will be departments who will not want to change, or collaborate—preferring you kindly-go-away so they can get on with their jobs. But as your transformation grows legs, there'll be less need for the task force to push. Instead, there'll be more check-ins and more requests for the task force to help departments and teams. This will be the tipping point, the one I referred to earlier—the point when departments will really start to operationalize the transformation, and momentum will begin to grow.

I worked with a large multinational African bank who decided that one of the most pivotal parts of their big platform transformation was going to be their risk department. Obviously, every bank is in the business of managing risk, so in a way it was very forward-thinking—and quite different, because normally everyone starts from customer experience. They thought about how they might transform risk digitally and where they might improve their processes via technology and automation—even considering artificial intelligence.

Even more importantly, they thought about how to change the mindset of their risk officers—who were both embedded in project teams and sitting at executive levels—to get them spotting opportunities to see risk in a different way as a bank. Normally, risk is a department that must adapt to what everyone else is doing. It was a very interesting and forward-thinking way to go about it. They took the parts of their bank that they thought might put them at the most risk during transformation, and put them forward as the ones to change the way they would think.

Decision four: revisit the choices outlined in your business case

When you make your business case to your Board, you'll make a number of key decisions and recommendations. For example, you may decide to start with one particular journey, like onboarding—but later, after you've considered your leadership, your transition model, and your principles, you might have a new understanding about how you're actually going to roll it all out that makes it worth revisiting some of your earlier decisions. Will that journey have been the right one to start with? Will all the other choices you'll have made by then impact the customer journey chosen? Did you pick the right one? An agile process is incremental by nature, so you should revisit choices regularly.

But, at the start of the implementation journey, it'll be a good idea to review all the choices you outlined in your original strategy as the task force is assembled—before you start to transform your first journey or process.

Choosing the right journey to start with is critical. Deloitte's banking maturity study of 2020 found a lot of banking digital leaders were getting traction for change from executive or Board stakeholders by concentrating on journeys that offered customers personal financial management tools, or focused on engagement drivers or sales boosters.[5] These digital leaders were often not focused on transforming fundamental journeys like onboarding. But, when they asked customers questions like:

"What would you like us to move from manual/in person to digital?" or *"What are the most important journeys for digital channels?"*

Their response was often very basic:

"I just want to be able to get a debit card within a couple of clicks."

They **did** want a simple onboarding journey.

This highlights a key decision you will probably want to revisit from your business case:

- Will your first changes focus on things you've never offered before, to give you lots of momentum and excitement within the bank?
- Or will you focus on the fundamentals your customers tell you they want?

Your first change could launch your transformation with a bang in the market:

"We're transforming personal financial management! We're going to be pioneers, we'll be like a Neobank and we'll lead the market."

Or, instead, maybe you'll decide:

"Our customers really just want debit cards online. It's a fundamental expectation they all have. We're going to transform that, because it'll give us a huge amount of engagement."

It really will be worth revisiting whatever original choice you make for your Board. I have seen presentations that made Boards excited because of cool new innovations. But later, it would come to light that what makes a branch teller excited is taking customers' pain away: No longer will customers need to come into branch, having completed six pages of "New Debit Card Form 2.1.6" and having spent hours looking for four types of ID ... and neither will the other 70+ customers a day who also come into the branch just to get a debit card. While this doesn't seem exciting on the surface, it delivers cost efficiency and customer satisfaction; fundamental pillars of shareholder value.

At some point, you may also want to reconsider principles originally defined for your task force.

If, for instance, you chose principles focused on them reducing operating expenses and simplifying operations, but in your Board presentation described journeys requiring huge amounts of capital or which would initially complicate the organization—you'll have immediately broken the task force principles and made it difficult for them operate.

As more data becomes available through your journey, revisit your decisions. Your task force not only needs to be very agile and flexible in the way they think, but also given the mandate by their Leader and the CEO to be able to change their strategy and roadmap.

Once you have everything set up and working with a Leader, a team, a set of principles, and success metrics, it'll be time to begin taking conscious pauses to keep your eye on the pulse, and check if you need to shift.

Time to ask yourself if you chose the right journey, and if all the parts fit and work together—and if necessary to revisit, adjust, fix, and then move on.

You may have presented a journey to your Board, but that doesn't mean you should be tied to it. In fact, changing it might be a good way for them to get them used to interfacing with you in an Agile manner. Things will shift—transitional tasks are unsuited to a normal Waterfall way of working. But you must understand that changes in working methods may be another difficult part of your bank's overall transition. Remember: if your Board signed off on one shape and then six months later want to find out how you're going with that shape, it will be super uncomfortable to only then say:

> *"Actually, we changed it into a totally different shape. But thanks for the money."*

And that segues nicely to your fifth key decision...

Decision five: how to communicate to the Board

How you communicate progress to your Board is critical and must be defined before you start your Engagement Banking transformation. It's often the piece of discipline that falls off first and leads to uncomfortable conversations when the money has already been spent.

Choose how and when you will communicate, and communicate your decision to the Board. You could let them know during the business case Board presentation when you ask for the money, but you don't have to. Instead it might be prudent to go back after 60-90 days and tell them about the critical choices you've made:

> *"This is who will be our Leader, this is the task force that we've put together and how they will work (organic/incremental or centralized), these are the principles the task force will operate by, and this is how we are going to communicate progress to you, the people who gave us the mandate."*

The choices to be made at this point are informed not by culture or DNA, but actually by how much data you have available inside the organization and how easy it is to get. Often you won't have the data to actually show benchmarks or progress as regularly as you would like. If you insist on making empirical data the cornerstone of your progress reports, you could inadvertently block the task force and make them focus so much on making sure they have good quality data before they report that they forget that they have other stuff to do. In Engagement Banking transformation, progress is always better than perfection.

Just start implementing and make the quality of your reporting and communication incrementally better over time.

When there is data available, be cautious about using digital dashboards or touchscreen digital boardrooms for the CEO and Board to monitor how the transformation is going in real-time—unfortunately, most executives and Board members don't know how to use them, and frankly won't have the time. Ultimately, they will rely on you keeping them informed in Board meetings. Transformation is a journey. Don't try to transform everything and everyone on day one. There are certain parts of your bank that are going to remain traditional for a while. Communicating regularly and using a language that the Board can understand is more important than using "Sexy Digital Tools."

For example: you'll probably create great success measures during your business case process. As your transformation journey moves into the sustainability phase, those success measures will likely become even more granular—and possibly move to an even more transformational level—because you'll start measuring different things. But at this pivotal stage, you need to translate them into the four fundamental pillars that your Board will care about: the shareholder value metrics:

- Revenue uplift.
- Operational efficiency.
- Asset efficiency.
- Expectations of the shareholders—and ultimately share price.

Keep in mind that if you tell them digital engagement is up by 60%, they won't know what it means:

> "*Is that good? Compared to what? Are we doing well? Did I spend the money well? Did we make a good decision? So we've got a conversion rate of 50%—what does that mean?*"

Be sure you're able to align every one of your new success measures to those shareholder value metrics. You'll save your Board the frustration of trying to make sense of a digital dashboard, and it will be much easier to talk to them on a quarterly basis. Even if you change the shape of your strategy, you should always tie it back to those key metrics. A difficult conversation with your Board about a shifting strategy becomes easier for them to swallow when you can say:

> "*When our strategy was shaped like this and it was all about the customer, these were our shareholder value metrics. We've changed the shape of our strategy and now we're going to go employee-first for these reasons—and here are the impacts on those same metrics.*"

Remember, you must speak their language, or the money will dry up; the Board will treat your bank's transformation as a program—and that program will end with you standing in front of the Board with egg on your face; another statistic as a failed transformation.

This point will be the beginning of a journey which will never end. Tell the Board what they need to know in their own language, using metrics they understand, and draw them into the transition with you.

Above all, manage expectations.

Think about the pace of a normal bank. Appointing a Leader and their team, deciding on the principles that they will work within and how they are going to work with the rest of the CXO, and how those principles are going to be measured, and what journey they are going to work on, and how they are going to interface with the Board is a lot to do in 90 days. Maybe that 90 day period should be extended to six months in a very big tier one bank—but the transition period should never be longer than that, or the planning will drag on, and making change happen quickly enough to keep everyone engaged will become impossible.

Avoid the ways banks fail

In my experience, banks who view Engagement Banking transformation as purely technological often fail in their attempt to transform. They tend to throw all of their budget at some very big pieces of technology and completely re-architect their core; but that doesn't solve every issue. I don't mean you won't need to review your core banking solutions; but that alone is simply not going to solve all your problems. Some banks have spent a massive amount of money on technology—designed and tested it in traditional ways—and ended up with a **slightly** more modern version of what they already had. With no processes or people shifted, and no KPIs in the bank changed, and no frameworks or job descriptions updated, but with a Board who've then said:

> *"These millions of dollars you've spent on this piece of technology—why does it not do what you'd promised?"*

Technology alone **cannot** deliver Engagement Banking transformation.

Other banks have made massive changes without understanding and considering the DNA of their organization. I once witnessed a Kenyan bank decide it would run their transformation as a "Speedboat"—a digital bank running alongside the main bank—without making changes to its underlying services which would be shared between the two—like HR and finance.

That meant some departments—HR and Procurement, for instance— had to serve both the old and new bank entities—whilst obviously being created for the legacy entity. But a **digital** bank **cannot have** a traditional bank's procurement office because of the agile nature in which a digital bank works. That bank saw the need for radical transformation, but tried to cut costs without understanding what a digital bank really needs to succeed. It brought the bank's entire digital transformation to its knees within six months. It took the bank much longer to admit to it.

In summary: there are two simple fundamentals you **must** understand and follow throughout your bank's Engagement Banking transformation. Failure to do so will put your bank at risk of failing to transform.

- **Fundamental 1:** transformation **will** flow through your entire organization.
- **Fundamental 2:** technology is **not** a silver bullet.

If you follow those two simple fundamentals, and the steps for the first 90 days as I've outlined, you'll set the whole of your organization on a journey that will transform your bank—into one your customers will love.

1. "Deloitte Digital Banking Maturity Report", Deloitte, October, 2020, https://www2.deloitte.com/content/dam/Deloitte/nl/Documents/financial-services/deloitte-nl-gx-fsi-digital-banking-maturity-2020.pdf
2. "Why Do Most Transformations Fail?", McKinsey & Company, July, 2019, https://www.mckinsey.com/~/media/McKinsey/Business%20Functions/Transformation/Our%20Insights/Why%20do%20most%20transformations%20fail%20A%20conversation%20with%20Harry%20Robinson/Why-do-most-transformations-fail-a-conversation-with-Harry-Robinson.pdf
3. "Designing the modern digital function", Deloitte Insights, January, 2021, https://www2.deloitte.com/us/en/insights/focus/industry-4-0/chief-digital-officer-digital-transformation-journey.html
4. "The New Elements of Digital Transformation", SLOANReview, November, 2020, https://sloanreview.mit.edu/article/the-new-elements-of-digital-transformation/
5. "Deloitte Digital Banking Maturity Report", Deloitte, October 2020, https://www2.deloitte.com/content/dam/Deloitte/nl/Documents/financial-services/deloitte-nl-gx-fsi-digital-banking-maturity-2020.pdf

Chapter 8

Culture: the driving force of your bank's transformation

Eric Berridge, Author; Executive Vice President, Salesforce; Co-host, Customer Obsessed Podcast

Watch a CEO address their employees, or read the opening to their annual shareholder report, and you'll recognize a familiar tune:

"At the heart of our success are our people and our culture. Our corporate culture sets us apart and gives us a winning edge."

Yawn.

Sorry if I sound like a cynic. But we've all heard it so much that it lacks any credibility without a reality-based context. As important as culture undoubtedly is to any organization's success, citing its importance as part of executive boilerplate-speak is meaningless. Executives and team leaders can't just stand up and talk about their great culture. It's one of those concepts and phrases that has devolved into corporate jargon, a "must-have" in any company communication.

Kind of like digital transformation.

It's essential for all business leaders to understand not only that culture is important, but also that establishing the **right** culture is the single most important thing to do in gaining customers—and in getting employees to go to the ends of the Earth on behalf of your company.

I like to refer to this as "cultural transformation" rather than "culture creation," since all organizations have some sort of culture to begin with. The challenge is understanding how culture can be transformed to meet new market conditions or adapted to reach new organizational goals.

As you can imagine, transforming an existing culture is really hard for many reasons not the least of which is human nature—our aversion to change. Especially when things seem to be going OK.

This understanding is particularly important in banking and other financial services sectors, where competition is greater than ever and new kinds of competitors—such as technology companies and consumer brands—have made serious inroads into the minds and wallets of customers.

It's also an industry where organizational culture has been cemented over time, making cultural transformation tricky—but essential.

Just consider the new customer reality banks must deal with:

People want simple, easy, immediate solutions to their problems—in **all** areas of their lives. The speed of digital transformation and the proliferation of digital-first experiences means that customers now expect **all** businesses to meet their highest standards of convenience, access, and service.

Don't be fooled into thinking the answer is just to use newer technology. As important as technology is—and it's probably even more important than you realize—without the right culture, you'll be left flailing on a tumultuous digital ocean.

There's a reason I titled my recent book *Customer Obsessed*, instead of "Customer Focused" or "Customer Driven;" it's because it is people, not products or technologies, that most disproportionately influence organizational success. Banks must act on the opportunity and imperative to build a culture based heavily on personal relationships—inside the organization and with customers—rather than on their products and services.

Customer obsession must be at the heart of your bank's culture. Without customer obsession, you might as well review the terms of your golden parachute—you're going to need it. But this isn't just another article, paper, or chapter about using your culture to improve customer service. It's one about getting the most out of your technology—and especially, your customer data—to build **preferred** customer relationships and drive **increased** customer engagement.

You can't do those things without a customer-obsessed culture.

Defining culture and its impact on banking

There are a lot of business consultants who make a lot of money advising organizations on how to set up a great corporate culture. But "culture" isn't always defined the same way, and it's not easy to recognize a **good** corporate culture unless you're really close to the action.

As you read this chapter, keep this definition in mind: I think of culture as meaning **how people come together to accomplish common goals.**

That's fairly easy to do when an organization starts with one leader, or a few visionaries who have a common idea of what to do and how to do it. The trick is upscaling that start-up culture. Adding people increases the complexity of maintaining and leveraging a culture exponentially, as do external factors such as competition, shifting customer needs, and new technology.

The thing that makes a strong, dynamic culture—and helps it hang together amid rapid and dramatic change—is the ability to create trust and human connections between both individuals and groups. A sense of trust and connectivity must hold true among employees—and between employees and customers.

This hasn't been easy for banks, whose corporate cultures focus primarily on their products and services. For decades, banks were really good at selling their products but really weak at understanding and anticipating their customers' wants and needs. They may have couched their expansions into areas like selling life insurance, writing mortgages, extending lines of credit, or offering wealth management consulting as "serving the customer," but all that was **really** about product line extensions. They often failed to build the trust and confidence that sit at the heart of customer-obsessed cultures, especially as customers' needs expanded and morphed.

Years ago, when we all banked locally and in person, that kind of trust-based culture was relatively easy to implement and experience. To open a checking account, apply for a car loan, or get a mortgage, we'd sit across the desk from a banker, and they would be our contact going forward. Of course, in those days, career longevity in banking was much more common than today, so there was a good chance that banker might become our de facto or actual "personal banker." If we had a problem, like confusion over a bounced check or a delay in getting a line of credit for our small business, we had someone to go to—as long as it was during the week, between the hours of nine and five.

I don't have to tell you how different banking is today: Full access, all the time, from any location or any device. Multi-channel. Digital-first. Convenience and efficiency over brand loyalty. If you do walk into a branch office, chances are there will be far fewer people working there; and it's unlikely you'll have built a trusted relationship with them.

Now, let's overlay some competitive challenges for banks and financial institutions.

It's undeniable that banks have plenty of company when it comes to competing for the loyalty and business of both consumer and commercial customers. Technology companies represent a daunting shift in the competitive landscape; research from Bain indicates that 54% of people trust a technology company with their money more than they do banks.[1]

Similar findings indicate that many of the world's largest and most successful retailers—Amazon, Walmart, Target, Costco, and others—have developed similar footholds in banking and financial services.

Banking's highly regulated, governance-driven nature has often tamped down innovation—in technology deployment, in banking operations and in cultural transformation. Undeniably, part of banks' vulnerability to these new competitors is due to culture—specifically, banks' tendency toward risk aversion. To be fair, that's understandable—entrusting one's money to a financial institution requires a lot of trust and confidence, and to some degree, a leap of faith.

Banks have always struggled to balance risk with opportunity, and too often have missed chances to innovate that would have helped them build a better experience for—and create a stronger bond with—their customers. Now, as those of us who have made our mark in the technology space know all too well, the road to innovation often comes with plenty of potholes. In fact, no innovative organization in **any** industry can be **truly** innovative without failing at least some of the time.

But the words "failure" and "risk" don't sit well in financial institution Board meetings...

So, how can we empower our cultures to embrace appropriate levels of risk and experimentation?

Data, culture, and digital transformation in banking

Remember my earlier point about technology companies and retailers becoming powerful competitors to traditional banks?

There's a good reason for it, and it relates to a common fabric for all those companies: data. Lots and lots of data, coming from countless devices, applications, clouds, and services. Tech firms and giant retailers are rooted in the cultivation and optimization of data, and using it in concert with their own customer-obsessed culture to gain a leg-up over old-school banks.

But banks aren't stuck entirely in their old ways; they also capture tons of data, and many use that data to influence everything from new product development to marketing strategies. They just don't do nearly as good a job as competitors from other backgrounds in **leveraging** that data, and applying it to further customer-obsessed cultures to benefit their customers and themselves. Insights from PwC state that only 37% of financial services firms said internal data and analytics will drive their next big decision.[2] Yikes.

Let me give you a real-world example: my own experience.

In my twenties, I moved to New York and went to a bank to open a checking account. To give you an idea how long ago that was, my primary goal was free checking, and I needed to open a CD account to get that. So I took $5,000—half my net worth at the time—and got my free checking.

Fast forward through the years. I got married, we had children, moved to the suburbs and bought a house, and eventually put our kids through college. Along the way, I started a company, grew it, and sold it.
At each of those steps in my life's journey, I was making transactions through my original checking account. Even with the sale of my company to IBM, the proceeds went initially into that account.

And how much proactive interaction did I have from my bank? **None**.

If my bank had used my data smartly, strategically, securely, and appropriately, they could have had a broader, deeper, and more successful relationship with me. I was generating tons and tons of data about my personal and professional life, creating a schematic of my wants and needs the bank could have used to inform and guide their engagement strategy—if anyone had taken the time to connect the dots. But because, like all other traditional banks, they were focused on selling their products and services to people walking through their branches, their culture—and their technology—did not focus on me and my needs.

Although organizations in many industries have embraced the data platform, banks and other financial institutions still struggle with the reality that most financial transactions run on and through the mainframe. And while the mainframe still offers a number of attributes such as security, resiliency, and institutional knowledge with in-house IT staff, banks are in the midst of a massive technology shift. This is why having a comprehensive, secure, and flexible data platform is essential to transforming your culture into a customer-obsessed culture.

Today, cloud computing is increasingly the platform of choice for new applications, especially those designed for environments like online banking, mobile banking, and software-as-a-service—all of which are well-understood and widely embraced by banks' customers. Data platforms designed and built for this new paradigm are marked by agility, easier scalability, and infinitely faster development and deployment. To use a software developer's lexicon, banks are used to "Waterfall" development, while the rest of the world has already embraced "Agile" development techniques.

Nimble companies thrive on rapid, incremental improvements that are rolled out quickly and iterated often. Technology companies roll out regular software updates to stay ahead of customers' needs and desires. This is the benefit of a cloud data platform—it enables rapid innovation for banks that put customer obsession at the center of their universe.

Banks today house massive amounts of data, and the growth of that data is accelerating every year. A bank with a customer-obsessed culture can use all that data to discover amazing insights about what customers need, why they need it, how they can use it, and how they are likely to want to consume it.

Also, modern platforms are designed with rock-solid security top of mind—which should comfort bank executives who worry about regulatory exposure, compliance mandates, identity theft, money laundering, ransomware, and a slew of other threats. That's because the data platform model is built on the concept of having all that precious, proprietary data in one place; not flying around the enterprise in static spreadsheets attached to emails.

Finally, the platform model makes it far easier and faster for employees to make decisions based on all available facts at any point in time. Remember the days of mortgage applications taking weeks or even months for review and approval? Or, in the following innovation wave, the technical hurdles customers had to jump through to either bank online or use a mobile banking application? Cloud-based platforms empower employees to make the customer's experience easier, with less stress and friction, while still maintaining the bank's commitment to security and privacy.

Building a customer-obsessed culture to drive engagement

I'm often asked a simple question about my book:

> *"Aren't all organizations obsessed with their customers—or at least trying to be?"*

The answer?

No, they're not. Not even close.

Far too many companies, including banks and other financial institutions, are obsessed all right—but they're obsessed with lagging indicators that they talk about with Wall Street and investors. They look at things that have already happened—revenue and profit reports, market share analyses, stock price... if those are headed in the right direction, bank leaders tell themselves (and their employees) that all is right with the world:

"Just keep on doing what you've been doing, and we'll all be fine."

That's a recipe for disaster—**and** it overlooks the critical role your employees play in shaping and presenting your culture to the outside world. Engaged employees create engaged customers, even if not all of your employees are in customer-facing roles. When your employees feel empowered to use customer and industry data to develop innovative solutions for customers' problems, customers ultimately benefit. When they do, the bank gets credit for being focused on the customer and not just in love with their own products.

You must figure out what drives your customers, what threatens them, what delights them. This is where your Engagement Banking platform comes into play: it's the laboratory in which problems and opportunities are identified, and where solutions are designed to build new, sustainable relationships of trust and increased engagement.

It's the platform that lets you know more about your customers. It won't be taking over the role of the branch manager, the familiar teller, or the loan officer your customers may still be dealing with, albeit on a more limited scale. It'll be extending what those traditional personal relationships relied upon—a shared understanding of what customers want and need, and of what their bank could and should deliver—and creating a scalable, repeatable approach built on a customer-obsessed culture.

A modern, future-proofed, cloud-based platform with open APIs, designed with easy accessibility for client-facing teams or for designing new solutions for individualized needs, is the way to go. The role of the platform is to help a financial institution know more about its customers than it could using data silos. It creates a culture of innovation, built around a customer-obsessed mentality.

If your customer data is walled off, opaque, difficult to access by non-technical employees or needs an already-overworked IT associate to run a one-off report, your data will move like sludge, instead of at warp speed. And when your team members can't get to the data and insights they need, they will become frustrated, unproductive, and unhappy. They will feel unfulfilled, unchallenged, and unappreciated. And they will leave, never to return.

Like a lot of your customers, I suppose.

But it doesn't have to be that way.

Banks have a unique opportunity to build a customer-obsessed culture that leverages the vast multitude of data they generate every day. That data is the basis for true insights that banks can use to do more than sell products and services. By running their data through machine learning algorithms that can proactively serve up recommendations to employees—based on how they interact with that data—banks can improve retention, and **turn clients into evangelists**.

It's the cultural transformation—a defined commitment to employees and customers—enabled by the platform, that makes the promise of digital engagement and transformation an exciting reality.

All views expressed are individual opinions of the contributor and don't represent the views, positions, or opinions of Salesforce.

1. "In Search of Customers Who Love Their Bank", Bain & Co., 2018
2. "Financial Institutions, Both Retail and Commercial, Have More Data on Their Customers Than Anyone Else", PwC, 2020

Proven techniques to gain executive buy-in to cultural Engagement Banking transformation

1. Frame your situational analysis, perceived challenges, and recommendations around business value. Then **back them up with data**. Make it a pragmatic, fact-based, and benefit-oriented discussion.

2. You need agreement on the key metrics and outcomes that measure success so you can report back to the C-suite and Board regularly and openly on progress. You need to get it up front, and you need maniacal clarity on what will affect those metrics. Get your fellow executives and the Board to sign up for them. There must be a candid discussion on the risks of not achieving the goals, and on the rewards of their being met.

3. Keep in mind that CEOs and other organizational leaders are not overly complex people with crazy needs and wants. In fact, the higher you go in an organization, the simpler people's goals usually are: increase sales and profits at a faster rate. Improve our competitive stance against new market entrants. Improve customer satisfaction and retention. **Keep your goals simple**.

Proven techniques to gain executive buy-in to cultural Engagement Banking transformation (continued)

4. Your best leaders will be the ones who understand that culture matters, and value both the concept of culture and its practice in the real world. They'll also likely be the ones who understand that savvy and appropriate use of an open data platform, when combined with a customer-obsessed culture, represents a worthwhile investment.

5. Remember the weight of cultural transformation cannot be carried by one executive or group alone. It is a team sport. It must be supported as a corporate initiative, with widespread involvement throughout your bank.

6. Share your progress. Don't miss opportunities to celebrate your wins—big or small. Stay transparent with your entire team, not just the higher-ups in the C-suite. If people can't see and feel the impact of their efforts, they'll lose any motivation to continue and stay true to the vision. But don't pad these report-outs with fluff. People can tell when you're being real and when you're pandering to them.

Five ways to gain employee buy-in to cultural Engagement Banking transformation

1. Change makes people uneasy, no matter how much it might benefit them now and in the future. You have to light the way forward for your employees and show them what's changing and what's staying the same. Clearly communicate the benefits, expectations, and timeline for any changes. And one more thing—don't overwhelm them. Focus on your top priorities, the two or three major shifts that are essential to your transformation. Cultural change has to happen gradually if you want it to stick.

2. You can inspire changes in your culture, but you can't force them. To gain buy-in and commitment from employees, identify key evangelists who are willing to adopt, model, and promote the technical, operational, and cultural changes you want to see spread throughout your organization.

3. Offer training. Train your people multiple times in multiple ways to give them a real opportunity to adopt new tech, processes, and behaviors. Everyone has their own learning style, so provide live training, a self-directed course, written manuals, video tutorials, a knowledge portal, regular Q&As— whatever you think your employees will connect with best.

Five ways to gain employee buy-in to cultural Engagement Banking transformation (continued)

4. People come first, technology comes second. Don't get overwhelmed by the tech specs of your transformation. When you focus on the real problems you're solving (and who you're solving them for) rather than the vast capabilities of the platform, you'll naturally narrow your focus, which will help you avoid tech bloat and scope creep. Don't let the shiny possibilities distract you from the goal: **customer obsession**.

5. Transformation depends on the strength of your vision and commitment. Before you launch any initiative, define the **why** and your solution's impact. Why does this transformation really matter? Who does it impact and who does it benefit? Why should people believe in it? Infuse your passion into the solution to inspire your employees and customers to embrace your Engagement Banking future state.

Chapter 9

The technology choices that empower change

Greg Fahy, Global Senior Vice President of Technology
Customer Success, Backbase

Yogesh Mulwani, Regional Vice President of Technology
Customer Success, Backbase

Technology continues to evolve at a breathtaking pace.

When this century began, the idea of billions of people having powerful, simple-to-use mobile computer and communications systems in their pockets was still the stuff of science fiction. Few could have imagined computing in something called "the cloud" would become pervasive, or that an online bookseller named Amazon would be the pioneer. There was no such thing as social media. Now, these technologies are deeply ingrained in the everyday fabric of life all over the world.

When considering digital technology it's always wise to expect the unexpected and be prepared for anything. As we've seen during the past decade, technologies such as mobile and cloud have disrupted many industries. Banking and finance have been deeply impacted, of course, but the pace of disruption and digital transformation in banking is now accelerating beyond anything the industry has seen before.

It is, in fact, revolutionary.

Customer demands are at the heart of the Engagement Banking revolution, but these demands are not being made in a vacuum. They are being made in an environment where digital technologies, interactions, and transactions have become ubiquitous—empowered by innovations such as cloud computing, open standards, mobile devices, and platform models.

If you're a banking leader looking to invest in digital technology to empower transformation, it's important to ask the right questions of your technology teams and potential partners. By doing so, you'll lessen the chances of your bank's initiatives being stalled or abandoned. With the right technology, you can deliver the flexibility, scale, and innovation in customer engagement the market demands. You can create transformative Engagement Banking applications, using a purpose-built, cloud-based, software-as-a-service platform that is secure, compliant, data-driven, and engagement-centric.

You can do all of those things. In fact, it's high time you got moving.

Technology is not only evolving at a breathtaking pace, but also evolving exponentially. The Engagement Banking revolution is happening all around you. Hopefully, your organization has already invested in foundational technologies such as cloud computing and open APIs. If it hasn't yet done so, there is still opportunity—but time is running short.

In this chapter, we look at the key technology decisions banking leaders must address to facilitate a shift to a customer engagement capability empowered by an engagement platform and infrastructure backbone.

We offer specific guidance on what to look for and why, and provide you with a checklist of key questions to ask your technology teams and potential partners to make your bank's digital journey as smooth, friction-free, and future-proofed as possible.

The single-platform approach

One of the most important technology decisions you should make early in the process is to choose the **single-platform model** as the foundation for your digital transformation journey.

What we mean by a single-platform approach is this: to provide a single foundation for all your data, services, channels, development cycles, and digital initiatives.

Focusing on the single-platform model will force your organization to properly analyze where it is and where it needs to go. It will make your organization confront and contextualize a shift in emphasis from an inside-out paradigm to an outside-in paradigm, whereby services and revenue models are driven by customer requirements and experiences, rather than by legacy business processes and systems.

Starting with the single-platform model will help you to define how technology will enable you to create a digital capability to continue delivering on your changing customer needs into the future. It will also be a key factor in determining if your organization can create that digital capability on its own, or if it will need a partner.

So, why should you choose a single-platform approach?

1. A single-platform will function as connective tissue between your digital engagement channels and your existing systems of record, as well as third-party FinTech services your customers are already using or would like to use.

2. By loosely coupling your existing systems of record with a single-platform, you will minimize risky adaptations to the monolithic systems you depend on for customer-critical applications and data. This will also create a faster path to innovation via a two-speed, outside-in approach—as Jouk describes in Chapter 3.

3. A single-platform will provide you with the flexibility, scale, and agility to adapt, and build new features and services in whatever directions are dictated by the market, your customers, and your business models.

4. A single-platform will provide you a single, consistent view of all data across all channels, and enable your organization to leverage consistent cybersecurity policies, procedures, and technologies across your entire ecosystem.

5. A single-platform will give all your developers access to these tools, technologies, and out-of-the-box applications, giving them the choice to build apps from scratch, or adopt pre-integrated apps when they need to go faster—and all while eliminating silos that stifle your innovations and digital transformation.

The reality is most banks are not in a position to build an engagement platform on their own, for reasons we will discuss below. By focusing on a single-platform approach, your organization will be able to determine what to look for in a partner. It will also guide your analysis for the best way to deploy, pay for, and scale the solution to foster innovation, new business models, differentiation, and new revenue streams.

As your organization goes through the process of determining what it needs from a single-platform, it will likely define requirements and set priorities and goals held fairly consistently across the banking industry, such as to:

- Eliminate silos between business units and services.
- Provide loosely coupled, seamless integration between your new Engagement Banking platform and existing systems of record.
- Provide seamless, friction-free integration with any relevant FinTech (or other) services, such as payments or credit, so your bank can be a one-stop hub for all financial services.
- Create a single 360° customer view that is current, complete, and consistent across all channels, accessible to everyone who needs it—including the customer.
- Ensure consistent data across your entire ecosystem to maximize the value of analytics, artificial intelligence, machine learning, blockchain, and other innovations to support an engaging customer experience and efficient operations.
- Leverage modern tools and technologies so your bank can react quickly and seamlessly with new features and services—at any time and at any scale.

- Provide a friction-free, simple, intuitive, data-driven experience for every aspect of customer engagement.
- Incorporate built-in security, resiliency, reliability, and trust on a future-proofed foundation that will allow for rapid innovation—without putting infrastructure and data at risk.

The technology foundation for a single-platform model **must** be cloud native and it **must** use open standards.

But before we get to that, let's address one of the questions that often comes up first in the boardroom and executive suite: build, or buy?

The build vs. buy decision

In order to innovate—and become a bank that people love—leaders are faced with a binary decision: whether to build... or to buy. Most banks are not in a position to build an Engagement Banking platform on their own. Even if yours could, would you want it to? Even if your bank is one of the largest in the world and has the money, personnel, and creative ideas to go its own way—even then, why would you throw resources at reinventing a lot of wheels that don't necessarily need reinventing?

Most banking leaders can't do that and don't want to. Especially given the new reality that they can use a purpose-built platform to provide the best of both worlds: the speed to move quickly **and** the flexibility to focus on differentiating the products, services, and business models that are most important to their customers.

First, let's look at time. It's of the essence. The revolution is under way.

If your bank chooses to build its own platform, you're probably looking at a good two years before you have the tech stack decisions, developer infrastructure, resources, and architecture foundation in place to start building features. Then you'll probably spend another two years redoing everything you did wrong the first time and adapting to the next set of changes that have taken place in the market. With this approach the opportunity costs and risk of losing existing customers is high.

Then there's the matter of personnel.

Yes: if your bank opts for a third-party Engagement Banking platform, you **will** need to hire digital teams to bring on new skills. You'll probably also have to re-train **some** of your current people. But a relatively small number in comparison with the hiring and training requirements of a do-it-yourself model.

With a third-party platform, you could control the amount of new hires by using the talents of your platform partner, particularly if your partner offers a managed services option. If you opt to build your own, however, you can take the number of new hires and multiply it exponentially. Even if you **could** find them in your region, you'd be up against the Big Techs and FinTechs in trying to recruit and retain talent, and the costs and risks will become glaring (and frightening).

Costs are another issue in the build-your-own model.

The capital expenditures will be enormous. Whatever you **think** it may cost when you get started, it will probably be double or triple that by the time you are done. And that's without considering you'll **never** be done, what with forever maintenance, upgrades, patching, servicing, security, and on and on and on.

You might be able to move a **bit** faster and with **less** strain on personnel by commissioning a black-label solution—in other words, commissioning a partner to design a platform specifically for your bank.

But this approach has significant drawbacks, especially when compared to a purpose-built third-party single-platform model. A black-label platform will be proprietary, which means it will be closed, and worse, expensive—perhaps even more so than a build-your-own model. And it won't just be more expensive at the outset. It will become even more expensive as your journey continues. Every time you want to make a change or upgrade, you will be reliant on that vendor to either do the work itself or provide the pathways for your team to do it. Either way, you'll pay the deluxe rate, even though you may not get deluxe value.

However, this technology decision isn't the "build or buy" binary one it used to be.

The top technlogy decisions

A single-platform approach, purpose-built, developer-flexible, third-party deployment model. That's the technology path. But not all technologies, solutions, and platforms are created equal.

As a banking leader, you should understand both what you need, and what you'll get from the technology when evaluating single-platform, purpose-built solutions.

Cloud-native technology and architecture

You don't want to be in the business of building commodity data centers. In fact, you want to unburden your organization from data centers wherever possible. Look for a platform that is built from the ground up with a cloud-native stack, rather than a lift-and-shift of traditional technology.

Organizations that are truly agile and customer focused are always in a position to safely and automatically deploy their software changes—and new customer value—without relying on an army of data center operations people and slow handoffs between teams. A cloud-native tech stack is a key enabler in leveraging the investment of your cloud provider in automation, reliability, security, resiliency, and scalability—leaving you to focus on delivering business value.

It is important to differentiate what you need for your **engagement platform** from what you need for your **existing systems of record**. For compliance or security purposes—or perhaps because of deep-rooted investments in proprietary applications—your IT teams may not be interested in, or even capable of, moving certain systems of record to the cloud.

What you need, however, is a way to loosely couple your Engagement Banking platform to ensure it has access **to** all the data in these applications, and that they in turn have access to the data they need **from** the Engagement Banking platform (see Figure 1). What's more, as the business scales and new sources of data multiply, you need to be able to offload workloads, data, and computing functions from the infrastructure supporting the systems of record and onto the engagement platform.

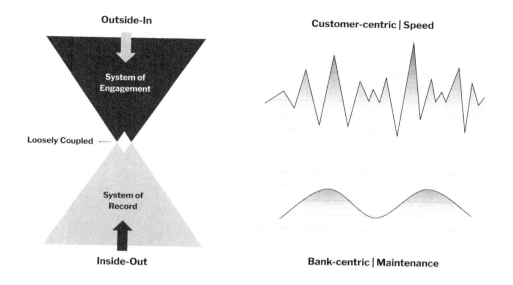

Figure 1: Systems of Engagement vs. Systems of Record—a loosely coupled architecture for innovation. Source: Backbase

This offloading will help to improve security and deliver scores of other benefits. For instance, the systems of record are where the customer transactions may be owned, but keeping it there rather than moving relevant data into the engagement platform becomes increasingly expensive. By moving data into the engagement platform, you reduce volumes on your existing systems. You also gain flexibility to enrich the quality of transactions, because the engagement platform brings all of the relevant customer data from all sources together in one place, thereby leveraging much richer data sets and unlimited scale.

Over time, the systems of record will focus on a narrower set of specific capabilities and the engagement platform will glue together and enrich those capabilities, making the entire ecosystem more efficient, automated, secure, scalable, and maintainable. It will also help you overcome some of the limitations of legacy applications and systems of record, and make it easier to migrate some systems of record to cloud models—if and when that becomes necessary and/or cost-effective.

You will now be able to operate with a two-speed model: slow for the systems of record, fast for the Engagement Banking platform. This will facilitate your bank's transformation from an inside-out model built on the systems of record, to an outside-in model—in which the Engagement Banking platform will give you the unprecedented speed and agility required for a new "heartbeat of innovation".

Open standards/open APIs

The technology to integrate your bank's engagement platform with its systems of record—as well as third-party services such as payments or credit card management —should be through an API layer that eliminates silos and provides seamless connectivity across your bank's entire ecosystem.

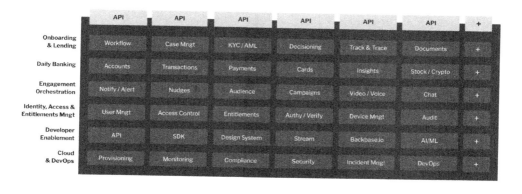

Figure 2: Engagement Banking Platform—the engine room of your engagement layer.
Source: Backbase

Even if you are bringing on net new customers through new digital channels, you still need to expose them and their data across all of your systems of record. When you put that layer in place, you have much more flexibility to decide which systems of record to invest in for the future and which to replace with cloud models.

Open standards are beneficial and necessary on a number of levels. For your IT and development teams, the friction to integrate is much lower. You can use industry-standard tools, take advantage of open-source frameworks and libraries, and make it easier (and faster) for developers to build new applications and features. When speed is of the essence, you can adopt pre-integrated apps to ease the pressure on your DevOps teams.

Also, you can more readily find and hire developers with the experience and skill sets you need. With open-source solutions and tools, you can use battle-tested knowledge and expertise. If something does go wrong, it is much simpler to identify the problem, fix it, and improve it.

If you choose the right Engagement Banking platform, you won't need to make that binary "build vs buy" decision.

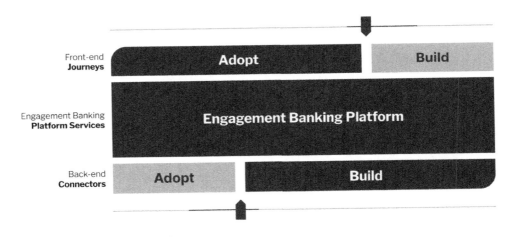

Figure 3: The Unique Differentiator. Source: Backbase

Cybersecurity

One of the challenges of modernizing cybersecurity is changing the legacy mindset of focusing on how security teams have worked in the past, to one of how they need to work now and into the future. The legacy mindset tends to a high level of trust in human- and paper-based processes.

That trust is usually misplaced and often leads to inconvenience for customers. There are more modern ways to handle security, and an open platform environment allows organizations to modernize and migrate cybersecurity to move with the times.

For example: with increased use of automation and sandboxed software development, your organization can integrate cybersecurity protections earlier in the development process. You can test in a meaningful way that's separate from your production environment.

You can also leverage the security, compliance, data sovereignty, and data privacy capabilities your cloud providers and/or software providers are building into their systems, so those become one less element for your organization to create or manage. You can take advantage of audited processes for GDPR or PCI compliance. You can have visibility across your entire environment, leveraging the security protections and personnel of your platform provider.

Scale, omnichannel capabilities, agility, trust

These capabilities are not a technology **per se**, but they **are** among the key outcomes of the technology choices you'll make. They are factors enabled by cloud technology and open platforms, and they deliver value that is essential to successful Engagement Banking.

The growth of digital engagements with customers creates an exponential increase in data—and a growing need to access all of that data for customer differentiation using deep analytics, and artificial and machine learning. You need a cloud architecture that scales to keep pace with the digital transformation of your customer engagements.

Another key requirement for customer engagement is omnichannel. Customers require a consistent experience across all channels—mobile, web, and even face-to-face. But that's not enough. When you evaluate the platform model, look beyond its ability to deliver a consistent experience; look for a solution that enables the channels to work in a unified, orchestrated fashion to enhance the customer experience.

For example, the biometrics on a customer's mobile device should work friction-free and seamlessly when they log on to the web. If they first log on to the web, it should work seamlessly when they next log on to their mobile device. If a bank employee can see exactly what the customer is seeing on any platform, they can service them in a way that is contextually aware. It's not just about omnichannel; it's about **engagement-enhanced** omnichannel.

Lack of agility has been a roadblock to digital transformation and is often a result of years of legacy cultures that have fostered siloed banking business models. Individual teams (say individual wealth management versus small business) have taken it upon themselves to build their own unique solutions for their customers. Silos get built when one part of an organization doesn't trust another. Often, these silos are difficult to tear down.

When you go for a technology reset, you must make sure you are creating a foundation trusted by people across your entire organization. If you lose the trust of your people, you risk them going off on their own, with their own infrastructure or public cloud solution; then you have a potential nightmare on your hands. Everyone using the same technical foundation is essential.

It starts from the top: not just by committing to the technology platform, but also by recognizing the importance of communication, culture, consistency, and confidence. We often tell customers it's easier to change software than change people. It's important to find a common groundwork for your people to embrace the technology. Otherwise, you risk having your technology investment go to waste.

Conversations between business and digital teams

As advocates of digital transformation—and as individuals with a strong commitment to technology as an agent of change—we have witnessed first-hand that it takes a certain amount of courage to embrace the kind of paradigm shift that we, and other authors, posit in this book.

For the most part, this book strives to deliver perspective to bankers and business leaders who are not necessarily technology specialists. We don't believe most of our readers have compelling desires to transform their banks into software or platform development companies.

But we do recognize that it takes something of a leap of faith to trust that the technology decisions you are making today, are the ones that will put your institution on the path to becoming a bank people love.

To make your leap of faith a bit less intimidating, and a lot more enthralling, overleaf you'll find a brief guide to some of the conversations you—as a business leader—should be having with tech teams and technology partners to benefit your Engagement Banking expedition.

Looking ahead

In today's world, digital platform technologies have become accelerators of exponential change. They have shaped—and continue to reshape—how we shop, where we eat, how we communicate, how we vote, how we consume entertainment, how we get information, how we travel, and how we access healthcare.

Digital platform technologies are now reshaping how we bank and manage our finances. The banking industry may not have been at the forefront of the platform revolution, but the revolution has arrived—and it is already creating enormous change in customer expectations and causing major disruption in traditional banking business models.

The technology to participate in the Engagement Banking revolution is available and easily accessible. Within a matter of weeks, **any** bank can use cloud computing, open APIs, and a purpose-built platform to accelerate its digital transformation.

The technology choices to empower change are before you.

This is not a time to be intimidated. It is a time to be decisive.

Ten tech questions for the Engagement Banking revolution

1. Does the platform use standard technologies and standard-based integration that can loosely connect to existing systems of record and third-party FinTech solutions quickly, easily, and securely? If not, why not?
2. How can a single-platform approach enable us to build around a customer-centric model versus a technology-centric model?
3. Can we identify friction in our customer journeys and how can we orchestrate specific technology—an engagement platform, systems of record, AI, automation—to eliminate friction at every touchpoint?
4. How can our technology choices reduce the time it takes to embrace and execute digital transformation, both at the front end and throughout the course of the journey?
5. Can we arm our employees with the right digital tools, and how easily will they be able to learn the platform so we can effectively deliver new products, services, business models, and innovations?

Ten tech questions for the Engagement Banking revolution (continued)

6. Regardless of the type of operating model we choose—can we find the digital talent we'll need?

7. Does the platform address all the key issues, such as performance, scalability, security, and resiliency to minimize risk in our digital transformation journey?

8. Does the platform provide a future-proof path, and can we have confidence that investments we make today will extend and scale as our digital initiatives grow and flourish?

9. If we partner with a third-party, purpose-built platform provider, how often will they update and upgrade the system and what kind of flexibility will they make available to our own developers?

10. How deep is the platform provider's marketplace and ecosystem? Will we have a range of choices as we look to continuously modernize to keep pace with the evolving needs of our customers?

Chapter 10

How the digital officer can drive sustainable Engagement Banking transformation

Andrew van der Hoven, Head of Digital and eCommerce
for Consumer and High Net Worth, Standard Bank Group

How did we get here?

It's important to understand how we arrived at this point, at which we recognize the value of, and need for, Engagement Banking.

Banks initially looked at digital in the early 2000's, as just another channel. A potentially more cost-effective way of distributing the same products and services to the same customer base. It was very much a supply-driven mindset.

In those first instances of digital transformation the predominant measure was:

> *"Have we moved physical transactions out of our branches, out of our physical infrastructure, into a digital world?"*

Unfortunately, this still seems to be the way banks around the world measure success. Banks that are thinking in this supply-driven, analog-to-digital way typically think of "percentage of transactions that are digital" as measures of performance. But eventually such statistics become relatively meaningless as performance measures, because the percentages are so high—after all, isn't banking mainly code?

So, does this really reflect meaningful change? What does "digital" mean in this context? Is it a format or method that makes sense to our customers, online or in an app? Or is it just someone's idea of how a former physical interaction might take place in a web browser?

We've had a real explosion of what can colloquially be called "web 2.0" companies like Google, Facebook, and Twitter—that is, digital-first companies that own and monetize data. A lot of these companies' business models tend to be based on aggregating peoples' **demand and interactions** in a digital way. When they aggregate this demand, it's often monetized and commercialized through advertising and marketing. But even more importantly, these companies convert customer demand into friction-free engagement and a deep understanding of what their customers desire. When you look at the way banks have traditionally done things, you see there's quite a big gap between this demand-driven versus supply-driven mindset.

These digital-first models tend to be very profitable because they can be replicated at digital scale at very low cost. Compare this to typical banks which are thinking: *"Customers come into my branch for an inquiry, how can I enable them to put in that same inquiry on an app or a web browser?"*

Traditional banks' supply-driven, straight-to-digital mindset must change.

Sustainable change

When banks stop thinking about very transaction-led digital interactions replacing physical interactions, and start thinking with a fully digitally enriched experience, they see they're in a great position to easily take advantage of all of its benefits:

- Banks typically know their customers quite well.

- They can offer very contextually relevant products and services.
- They can easily connect to customers with clicks, rather than with physical interactions.

So many banks are simply not taking advantage of this. But for those banks that are, how do we make the change in a sustainable way? That is, in a way that enables and supports growth across their entire ecosystem? My definition of sustainable is: when value is created on both sides— customer and provider.

At a high level, we must:

1. Change our overall mindset away from a purely transactional relationship that's simply happening digitally.
2. Utilize all the benefits a digital platform and digital technology can truly offer.
3. Ensure that measures are aligned to those outcomes.
4. Think about the new business models this might enable us to take forward.

These measures are necessary to sustain movement from a very transaction-focused model to one with much more engagement and demand. This will allow us to utilize the full power of digital, very much like the "best-in-breed" platforms do.

Based on the data we see, **people are typically much more engaged with their banks than with many startups and digital-first**

companies. For example, some of the best banks in the world are seeing almost 50% of their monthly active users log into their apps daily. This is **incredible engagement!** Many digital-first companies would kill for that level of consumer interaction. And yet, too many banks are seeing almost zero benefits of this degree of engagement because of their outdated mindsets.

How do you achieve the right mindset?

Boards and senior leadership in most banks have grown up in an analog world, where digital is just a cost-reduction mechanism and not an engagement mechanism. How do you change that mindset in your bank?

The first step is to help your executives understand that the market in which their customers exist is no longer defined by banking products. It's actually defined by "share of attention." Your customer is no longer a "home loan customer" or a "credit card customer." Instead, they are a customer that is actively engaged—or not.

It's important to understand that this new digital relationship means that your competition has changed as well. Once you exist in a relationship with your customers digitally—via your app or web platform—then you are competing with anybody else that has an app or some sort of digital service. Look at how many of the big digital-first companies define their market. They don't define it as making connections with others. Facebook, for example, defines their market as all of their consumers' attention. We all have a limit to our attention span and there are only so many hours in a day we can be on our screens.

The Board and senior executives need to recognize that people are spending more of their time digitally. That means it's their share of attention that you're going after—not the old banking metrics of share of wallet and share of financial relationship. You are competing just as much against TikTok as you are against other banks. People only have two eyes and 24 hours in a day. How much of their time are they going to spend with your bank?

How can you get your senior leaders to realize their mindset needs to be different?

You can start by gathering data about how much time people are spending digitally and what they are spending it on. It's widely available. Then compare it to your own statistics. We've done this exercise a few times with executives and it's quite surprising how much time people actually spend with their banks digitally. But it pales in comparison to how much time people are spending online in all other manners of contextual platforms. Looking at those numbers can be quite an eye-opener!

Then, using your own data and your own set of standards, define some new engagement measures. You might not immediately fit targets to your new measures, but you can observe them and come to understand them. How many hours are people spending with you? What are they spending it on? Are those hours converting into some sort of tangible revenue? If not, why not? If your interactions are quite frequent but very short, then immediately you know you have a brief transactional relationship with your customers. It's those measures that you'll find value in tracking over time.

Once you've tracked those metrics, you can start asking questions like:

"How do we commercialize this?"

"How do we drive this in a sustainable way?"

You'll usually find the answer is to personalize and contextualize a lot more. You need to help people solve real-world problems. The competition is just a click away.

How do you build sustainably?

So, let's say you've managed to change senior management's mindset. They are starting to rethink the market and who the real competitors are. You've started to track some basic metrics at a very high level—such as time spent on your Engagement Banking platform and conversion rates over number of visitors. You're already seeing data which suggests you're not appropriately utilizing the time you have with your customers.

What's next?

It's important to start small. Choose a part of your customers' experience where you can provide a lot more contextual, personalized interactions.

Choose ones that you hope will influence the metrics you're monitoring by solving particular customer problems. It could even be making a change to a poorly built digital function.

Let's use the example of your website. You may be surprised to find that not every page is mobile responsive—sometimes some of the most important pages are not. Imagine what happens: your customers are browsing your website on their mobile device, and they can't actually take action because they can't find the button. It's simple things like that which can cause a lot of harm.

Your first steps, then, are to choose a category; set very clear improvements; measure a baseline for that category—like conversion, or some other engagement metrics, like how many people visit, how often, for how long—and set yourself an improvement goal for it. Once you dive into those funnels and understand how your customers are flowing through their journey, you'll very quickly come to understand what the key problems are. The changes that make the biggest impact are often not big digital transformation changes. They are practical changes in your flow that take the friction out of the customer journey.

This is how you build sustainably. It's not about going wide; it's about going deep. It's not about changing the whole bank and the whole mindset. It's starting with changing a little bit of the thinking, and then going deep within a category of understanding or product or whatever it is that your bank is specifically good at, and seeing if you can influence customer outcomes in a positive way. You have to remember to redefine your market, who your competition is, and what engagement means to your customers.

It's also about making this a cross-functional mission, not just something one team is working on. This is a cultural shift. Teams made up of members from different parts of the bank—engineering, product, digital, marketing—aren't something that's deeply ingrained in banks' cultural DNA, but they are what is needed to solve these customer problems.

Another cultural shift is how the bank thinks about engineering. In general, financial institutions think of it as a cost line, not a business value. There is a bit of irony in the whole "digital transformation." Someone said to me the other day:

> *"Everything I do is digital! That means it must happen in your area."*

> And I said: *"No, no, guys, digital is a capability. It's not someone owning this."*

Effectively digital is not a destination, it's a capability—we all own this together. Digital-first companies understand that digital isn't just the realm of engineering—now it's just business. It's how all teams get things done.

Ultimately, you have to understand that (in the words of Marc Andreessen) *"Software is eating the world."* Digital has grown. But many still don't necessarily realize that the cost of software distribution is getting close to zero. This means the cost of distribution of services to your customers is also close to zero—and so distribution is no longer a barrier to entry. You now have a tremendous opportunity to commercialize.

Think about new business models

Engagement is very much a demand metric and a demand way of thinking. **On the internet, the most prosperous are not the ones with the supply of products and services. It's those with demand. It's those who can capture and monetize demand.**

Banks have been really bad at that because we've got supply, we've got lots of products, we've got financing, and in a way we're just waiting for customers to come. What we're not great at is demand, generally. How can we think more like a FinTech player, with their understanding of how to incentivize more sign-ups?

This is the time to think about new opportunities and new ways of doing business to take advantage of both what we're good at and the promise of digital engagement.

One thought is to consider new revenue streams based on our huge number of banking partners and meaningful professional relationships. Bank partners and business customers can become extensions of the products and services offered by your bank, aggregated and connected to provide solutions for customer problems. Your bank could disintermediate all sorts of transactions currently happening on other platforms and increase margins in the process—for example, the buying and selling of goods.

Think about it: banking might not just be current accounts any more.

There's also a huge opportunity around learning about your customers—which might lead to new ideas about business models, and to solving problems for them, gaining even more engagement. Take acquisition, for example. The internet is an amazing vehicle for acquiring and understanding customers—if used correctly. It has a far a lower acquisition cost than any other measure. Why? Because if you put up a billboard, and later you're sitting in one of your branches, you don't know if a person walking into the branch has seen that billboard and thought, *"That's great, I want that product,"* or if it's just because of some other random interaction. With digital, you know immediately what works and what doesn't. You can test and change fast, and you can quickly identify issues and solve them for your customers. You can learn about what your customers want, and like, and need—and adapt to it.

All that said, it's important to be ethically sound in the methodologies that you follow. We're still operating in a broader margin where customer journeys have huge room for improvement. We don't need to use questionable techniques to trick our customers into engaging with us—our job is simply to help them get the solutions they need. Remember to hold integrity, trust, and the other familiar principles of banking quite clear.

Technology and partnerships for success

You don't need to make large technical investments to start making changes. But if you're doing it right, you'll quite quickly reach a point when you will realize that you don't have the flexibility that you need. The best methodology is one that allows the teams and the work to define what happens next. That way, whatever does happen doesn't become an imposition which everyone "has to live with." What I've seen is that many of our systems were just never designed with flexibility in mind. Core banking systems from the last 20-30 years were never designed to enable people to have multiple ways of thinking about accounts—like family accounts—let alone new ideas about customer engagement. They were designed to be stable, long-term systems. They weren't designed to adapt to the digital engagement model.

You could carry out a large replacement of existing systems with one of the new cloud-based core banking platforms, but you can do a great deal well before you get to that point. You can achieve the agility and flexibility you need with a number of different partners—one of the market leaders being Backbase.

Don't think you can do it yourself. Partners are important, not just because they might provide you with the technical systems to enable what you need, but also because they are growing and developing too. They understand the world and the limits of their own technology, and a partnership means they can share these insights with you.

To keep your progress sustainable a fire needs to be ignited internally—but **you can't keep it burning by yourself.** Eventually, in a way, you'll run out of firewood. **You need help from partners**.

When considering a potential technical partner, keep these things in mind:

- The partner must be sustainable and have longevity. Banks have existed for hundreds of years, so you must think about being in a partnership for a long time. You don't want the next startup to just pop up and give you a different solution. You want a partner that you can rely on in the long term.
- Your partner needs to share your methodology, or belief in the way that the world is going. Banks typically implement SAFe (Scaled Agile Framework) – which is useful but not great. In a way, it treats engineering team members as factories, which means it's likely lived past its usefulness. You need a partner who believes it's all about the people on both sides, not just the methodology.
- Your partner should have the highest technical standards possible. High technical standards are great—almost like a ticket to the game in a way. It's about future vision.
- A really good partner will challenge you to some extent, not just be "yes men." You are likely coming from a place of risk aversion and safety, so you want a partner who is going to challenge you and educate you.
- And finally—a good partner must be willing to do the hard work and give your team room to focus on innovation.

Important considerations

There is one point I once read that has really stuck with me: if you treat Engagement Banking change as a **transformation**, you always create winners and losers.

That mindset immediately draws battle lines within an organization, culturally. This is why I advocate a more start-small, test-and-learn type of approach. It doesn't immediately polarize an organization. Instead it enables people to learn and go. It also gives people the freedom to know that they don't have to know everything. There's no magical "transformation office" that is going to somehow wave their magic wand and make us all feel a lot better about the world. The approach you take must take into account that many people are learning brand new skills.

You want to make change happen "in the work." This is a phrase that we use quite often. You don't want the transformation to happen outside of the work and be imposed or enabled by others. You want the teams **in** the work to do it. Decisions should naturally evolve. If you're doing it right, it's far more likely you'll end up with a completely different business model and a different way of thinking, born of many small experiments, than it would be if someone at the top had made the decision to turn left or right. You have to hold that space for teams.

What things make the process more, or less sustainable?

- Big transformations, or changes that are driven from the top down, are less sustainable. Think of starting small, with teams, instead. Let the change flow out from the teams doing the work.
- The process will be much less sustainable if you don't realize there will be cultural changes at the same time. Deliberately work on culture. Remember, banks tend to be functional to the core, so create cross-functional teams who will work to solve customer problems or drive engagement.
- If you expect things will be the same and happen in a functional way... they won't. You need to break some of those functional things up—and maybe break a couple of "rules" around that.
- Because of the need for cultural change, we often underestimate the people impact. You can't continue to apply the old bank manager grading and team-based systems. Realize instead that grading and remuneration are part of the same system, and consider changing them to be almost "team-first" rather than focused on the individual.
- Thinking in terms of quarterly earnings and quarterly metrics is less sustainable, especially when it comes to the smaller teams you need. More sustainable is to give teams space to learn and set their own outcomes—based on some guidelines, of course.

Finally, my advice for a leader who is approaching this change:

First, don't expect it all at once. People tend to expect this magical moment when everything is just going to change, which just doesn't exist in reality. It's a long, hard slog. The more you're in it, the more you understand that there's no real "change moment"—it's just what you do.

Second, realize there's a huge cultural component, and you're going to have to do a lot of hard work on that.

Last, start and maintain a dialogue. Explain to leadership who you're competing against and how you are thinking about it, and how the mindset needs to change. Then you can start. But remember – start small.

Leading the revolution

Thomas Fuss, Chief Technology Officer, Backbase

The last words of *The Engagement Banking Revolution* fall to me.

And it's an honor to write them.

What all of us at Backbase—and I personally—most want to convey to our readers, customers, and potential customers is that the journey we're all taking together is **exciting**. Actually, it's more than exciting—it's exhilarating and enlightening; and if we're fortunate, it'll also be fun and rewarding.

There have been a lot of smart things said by a lot of smart people in the preceding pages. About digital transformation; digital disruption; the value of platform models; the importance of customer engagement; the vast potential that technology offers for business innovation in banking, and the rare opportunity to reimagine our operating models.

All of us in banking are being given the chance to change an industry; to innovate, to make people's lives better. It's not a time for complacency or maintaining the status quo. It's a time for action; for decisiveness; for **creativity**.

So, I ask you this: what more can you want from the work that you do, the years of training you've put in, but for your knowledge, experience, and expertise to be put to good use?

> *How about the chance to do something special that will have a lasting impact on the world?*

Connecting with customers through digital transformation

Connecting with customers, listening to their views, solving their challenges, and inspiring them to be bold and innovative are running themes in this book. They also embody a philosophy and practice I have strongly adhered to in every role I've ever had in the banking and technology industry.

When I talk to our customers today, one of the things they most want to talk to me about is digital transformation. Not just because I am, after all, the Chief Technology Officer of a company that offers digital transformation solutions—but because Backbase approaches digital transformation **differently**.

Here are some of the things we talk about:

> **Digital transformation is here to stay, and it is a never-ending journey:** This is one of the reasons I love working in the space we're in. We'll be continuously confronted by ongoing challenges that will test our creativity, courage, skills, and knowledge. We'll never be bored; we'll always be engaged. I believe that has to be the mindset of any leader in the modern digital banking space. While digital transformation is an enormous challenge, we will not be daunted by the challenges we'll face. We will embrace the unknown, rather than being intimidated or overwhelmed.

Digital transformation is a marathon, not a sprint: Banking leaders in the executive suite, in the boardrooms, or on the front lines in the IT or digital departments are under a lot of pressure to make transformation happen—and make it happen fast. But you don't have to change everything all at once. You can stretch the transformation you need over time, focusing on meeting key goals that continuously push the process forward.

Digital transformation is more about the human than the product: One of the common mistakes people make is to get amped up by technology and try to find a purpose for it. It must be the other way around—you must marry the technology to the problem you are trying to solve for the customer, or to how you are trying to reduce points of friction.

Here's an example. A recent study by McKinsey & Company concluded that about 70% of investments in artificial intelligence (AI) in banking produce no yield—partly because the banks lack a clear strategy for AI.[1] Yet, the report also notes that AI can help boost revenues across more than 25 use cases. We simply have to be more intelligent about how we use it.

Addressing obstacles to customer Engagement Banking

Not every customer I talk to immediately says *"Yes"* to digital transformation or Engagement Banking. Of course, I think this is a mistake, because I believe in what I do and that it has a higher purpose. So, I talk to them to try to uncover their objections or concerns.

Typically, hesitation is a matter of priorities. There are banks out there that still haven't made digital transformation their absolute top priority. Sometimes this is because they are focused on cost optimization, which a lot of financial institutions are actually built around. I must emphasize: **digital transformation is an investment in the future. It will not help to optimize your P&L for the next quarter.**

The Big Techs in Silicon Valley view that shortsighted attitude as a weakness and a vulnerability. When banks think that way, and decide to focus more on short-term financial statements and less on a long-term, customer-first vision, they are playing into the hands of those Big Techs. It only makes them even more aggressive, and even more confident that they can move in and create disruption and devour market share.

Other objections I often hear from customers are:

> **Digital transformation is too hard:** Regardless of the channel they're using to connect with their bank, the average customer experiences a highly fragmented journey. And that experience might be very different from one channel to the next— further infuriating

the customer. For the bank, maybe it's an intimidating technological challenge adapting legacy systems, shifting to cloud operating models, removing silos, and creating a unified customer view across all channels. But there's no longer any reason for that challenge to feel intimidating. An Engagement Banking platform can be loosely coupled to your existing systems of record to fuel your innovation and ability to launch new lines of business, and engage your customers and employees.

The war for talent is real, and banks are not on the winning side: Compounding the difficulty of digital transformation is the simple reality that there is a shortage of IT talent. Ask any CIO in banking today. They will tell you their biggest challenge is people—specifically, technology talent with the right expertise and skills, in areas such as cloud computing, cybersecurity, DevOps, AI, and more. So why not use the right technology partners and a unified Engagement Banking platform? One with the APIs to connect to your existing systems of record? One with out-of-the-box applications **and** custom app development to build your own unique features? Wouldn't that be better than trying to further compete in an overly aggressive war for talent to build your own platform from scratch?

Using the right technology partners and the right platform will enable you to focus on your core business—and on making your bank one your customers love.

Their banking leaders have deeply ingrained habits or are simply complacent: The simple truth is some people in banking are comfortable with the way things are and don't want them to change. For them, it's much harder to be bold than to keep old and comfortable habits and behaviors. Frankly, this is one of the hardest barriers to overcome—because it's emotional, not logical.

Let's be clear: digital transformation is happening whether you participate or not. It's what your customers expect, and if you don't give them satisfying and engaging digital experiences, they will simply go somewhere else without the slightest regret.

At Backbase we have the Engagement Banking platform to help customers take on most of the difficult tasks involved in transforming to an Engagement Banking model. We empower them to speed both innovation and delivery by adopting our powerful out-of-the-box applications, while providing them with the flexibility to develop their own unique apps as required. We also have the right people already in place so our customers don't have to participate in the war for talent. As for the challenge of breaking complacency—well, we're doing our best to make transformation easy and stress the importance of moving forward. We hope this book you are finishing is evidence of that.

The steps to take towards truly engaging your customers

Now that you and your teams are as excited and exhilarated as we are by the Engagement Banking revolution, how do you translate that into action?

As you've read in this book already—you start by trying to understand who your customers really are and then set about creating the bank for those personas. Once you discover what you need to make the bank personal for each customer, then the technologies will fall into place.

When I was working at a bank, we discovered a disconnect between who we were trying to attract as new customers and what they **actually** needed. We created products by looking at our stickiest customers and the ones who were driving the most revenue. For the most part, these were established, mid-life customers and our offerings were geared to fit their needs.

But we were trying to bring on new customers who were recently out of school: young professionals. We had the wrong offerings. When we looked at the personas, it was a real eye-opener. Sometimes the customers you have now may not be the customers who are going to be necessary for your future.

You need to drive engagements based on all of your customers. You need to create personas with at least 20 data points each: age, income, education, family status, marital status—all of the standard points you would look at. But you have to go deeper. For example, look at how people behave and operate, and personalize services for them.

If someone is a self-informer, they will look for quick actions. If someone seeks a lot of advice, you will have to engage with them at a much higher, more consistent, more informative, even more intimate level. The way you engage is a determinant in the way you deploy the technology in terms of:

1. Which channels you use and how.
2. The frequency with which you engage.
3. The type of content you deliver to each customer.

The technology platform you use for engagement must have the flexibility to be loosely coupled to your existing systems to let you personalize your offerings for each customer. At the end of the day, you need to be enabled to confidently innovate, reach out, build connections, and deliver engaging content on every channel—without being restricted by the rigid systems of record which provide your customer-critical data and applications.

It's about being able to integrate all channels consistently as needed at any moment in time. It's about bringing all the pieces together, including aggregated information that may come from another bank or a FinTech. It's about creating digital moments when they are most impactful and meaningful for the customer—not necessarily for the bank.

Another important point I share to help customers start their journey successfully is to focus on creating value for their customers, and not waste time on re-inventing the basics. Simplify, and concentrate on the things that really matter. For example, every bank will say it's unique, yet when you open their apps, they all have a login page. Why reinvent the wheel? Don't re-invest in creating the most compelling login page; instead, spend your time thinking about how you can manage the accounts to achieve competitive advantage and thrill your customer.

Customer engagement in banking: looking ahead

COVID-19 has been a disruptor in all of our lives. It's also been an accelerant in making our world more digital and making people more reliant on digital technologies and connections.

Even as the world continues to evolve, I believe that engaging with customers still comes down to something very simple: people want to know it's about **them**. Fortunately, the technology to do it is there. We are in a position to open up new possibilities and touchpoints for engagement to improve people's lives.

When I think about the future, I think of invisible banking. Perhaps it starts with an invisible assistant—like an Alexa or Siri—that proactively offers us choices without any human interaction. Eventually, the customer shouldn't have to take any action at all. Their bank would have all of their information. They would know all the customer's goals, priorities, and proclivities, and always act in their best interests. This service level already exists in wealth management—the richest people in the world probably rarely speak to a financial advisor; the advisor is trusted to act in their interest.

Perhaps the Engagement Banking revolution in its current iteration isn't ready for that level of sea change quite yet. But we are laying the groundwork for advances and innovations to allow us to engage with customers in ways never before imagined.

You can view the revolution with trepidation; Or you can embrace it with passion and enthusiasm, as I do. I see us at a starting point. We have a unique opportunity. Not only can we **envision** the future of banking—we are also in a position to **shape** it.

Shaping the future of Engagement Banking

And so, we come to the end of this particular journey. The closing section of the closing chapter of the first book to comprehensively define, chronicle, and set forth a vision for the future of banking—specifically, the Engagement Banking revolution. We at Backbase hope that this book will be of service to all of us in the banking industry—whether it's as a start point, or as an important step for those further along on their journeys.

Before us, we have the rare opportunity to participate in reshaping an industry to improve quality of life for ourselves and our customers. As I said at the outset: at Backbase, we find this opportunity exhilarating and exciting.

But we didn't create this book just to share **those** feelings. We also felt it imperative to communicate our sense of the urgency of the mission at hand.

Make no mistake: banking is in the midst of a paradigm shift that **will** take place—whether you choose to participate or not. As our founder and CEO, Jouk Pleiter stated in this book's preface: It has been designed as a guide; a playbook. Not just a book about why Engagement Banking is necessary, but one that shows you **what you can do about it**.

For example:

- You can ensure that your teams understand the power of platform models and what they need to consider in building a platform strategy, based on the expertise of Sangeet Paul Choudary in chapter two.
- You can follow the advice of Heidi Custers in chapter seven to ensure that your Engagement Banking platform is successful.
- You can elevate to higher value Contextual Banking and Conscious Banking models as described in the Banking Reinvention Quadrant by Paolo Sironi in chapter four.
- Use Jouk's advice in chapter three to take your bank into the new world of banking. Begin with the ending—define the everyday problems your bank will solve to become a bank people love.

Each chapter provides practical guidance you can use to make changes necessary to evolve your bank; to move from legacy, spaghetti, inside-out design thinking, to a unified, open, cusotmer-centric, outside-in single platform ecosystem.

Any bank that does not embrace this change and focus on engaging with the customer is not merely endangering its future as a viable institution: it's setting the stage to write its own obituary.

Backbase is the **only** company that has an Engagement Banking platform designed to make that journey as personal, seamless, simple—and dare we say, exhilarating—as possible.

Our mission is to relentlessly innovate to empower you to achieve our shared vision for the future of banking.

1. "AI-bank of the future: Can banks meet the AI challenge?", McKinsey.com, September 19, 2020, https://www.mckinsey.com/industries/financial-services/our-insights/ai-bank-of-the-future-can-banks-meet-the-ai-challenge

Biographies

Eric Berridge

Author; Executive Vice President and Commercial Officer, Salesforce

Eric is the author of several best-selling books, including *Customer Obsessed;* and was Co-Founder and CEO of Bluewolf, an IBM Company (acquired in 2016)—a firm he built over two decades as the original and preeminent consultancy for Salesforce. Eric has also been a TED speaker, and co-hosts the Customer Obsessed podcast.

Sangeet Paul Choudary

Author; Founder, Platformation Labs

Sangeet has authored several best-selling books, including *Platform Revolution* and *Platform Scale*. He has advised the leadership of more than 40 Fortune 500 firms and was selected as a Young Global Leader by the World Economic Forum in 2017. Sangeet is a frequent keynote speaker, regularly addressing leading global forums including the United Nations, the World Economic Forum, and G20 and World50 Summits.

Heidi Custers

Digital Transformation Director for Middle East
and Africa,
Backbase

Throughout her career, Heidi has focused on championing customer-led digital transformation for companies such as Deloitte Digital, 42Engines, and Standard Bank. Since 2006 she has been working with leading African enterprises to guide them through the various aspects of their digital journeys.

Greg Fahy

Global Senior Vice President of Technology
Customer Success,
Backbase

With over 20 years of experience in architecting cutting-edge technology solutions, Greg applies his deep expertise in cloud strategy, digital product management, and Agile software development to help banks transform their legacy siloes into customer-centric experience, and accelerate growth.

Thomas Fuss

Chief Technical Officer,
Backbase

Thomas gained his experience in software engineering and digital transformation at ING Bank, and by co-founding Payconiq, the payment platform. Thomas is responsible for driving numerous digital transformation programmes and pivoting native cloud technologies to accelerate the development of next generation Engagement Banking solutions.

Ben Morales

Chief Technology Officer and Operations Officer,
Washington State Employees Credit Union

Ben Morales is chief technology and operations officer at Washington State Employees Credit Union. In a career spanning more than 30 years, he has held numerous leadership positions in the credit union industry, and co-founded QCash Financial, a leading credit union service organization.

Yogesh Mulwani

Regional Vice President of Technology
Customer Success,
Backbase

Yogesh has worked in the technology industry for more than 20 years, building digital platforms and leading large-scale technology transformation initiatives for enterprises. Yogesh has spent the last ten years working within financial services to improve customer experience across digital channels.

Jouk Pleiter

Chief Executive Officer,
Backbase

Jouk founded Backbase in 2003. Previously he was President and Co-Founder of Tridion—one of the world's leading WCM software vendors—which was later acquired by SDL and renamed SDL Tridion. He also co-founded Twinspark Consultancy, one of the first interactive web agencies in the Netherlands. Jouk holds a Master of Business Administration degree from the University of Groningen.

Tim Rutten
Senior Vice President of Strategy,
Backbase

Tim realized his passion for digital entrepreneurship the moment he gained access to the internet, and started his first business. A Bachelor's in Economics and a Master's in International Business took Tim to the Kauffman Global Scholarship, which in turn took him to Harvard, Stanford, and MIT.

Paolo Sironi
Author; Global Research Leader,
Banking and Financial Markets,
IBM Consulting

Paolo is the author of several best-selling books, including *Banks and Fintech on Platform Economies*. He is one of the world's most respected FinTech voices. Executives in financial institutions, start-ups, and regulators all around the world benefit from his business expertise and strategic thinking.

Andrew van der Hoven

Head of Digital and eCommerce for Consumer
and High Net Worth,
Standard Bank Group

Andrew is a dynamic financial services executive with over
20 years active involvement in shaping and deploying digital
strategies, building and leading product roadmaps, and
mentoring agile cross-functional product teams.

Mayur Vichare

Head of Value Consulting,
Backbase

During his career, Mayur has worked with Fortune 100
companies to develop end-to-end customer journeys and
platform models to drive strong business value. Mayur
brings deep experience in developing innovative digital
solutions across a diverse range of sectors, including the
FinTech and banking spaces.

Bibliography

Backbase. "Customers are in control." https://www.backbase.com/citizens-case-study-connect-2019/.

———. "Jouk Pleiter keynote presentation: Engage 2022." November, 2021. https://fast.wistia.net/embed/channel/355q8nsxx8?wchannelid=355q8nsxx8&wvideoid=fjphcgshw9.

———. "Modernizing Techcombank for a digital transformation." https://www.backbase.com/best-bank-in-vietnam-techcombank/.

———. "Study shows growing gap between German customer expectations and digital banking offerings." November, 2021.

Bain & Company. "Banking's Amazon Moment." March 05, 2019. https://www.bain.com/insights/bankings-amazon-moment/.

———. "In Search of Customers Who Love Their Bank." 2018. https://www.bain.com/contentassets/7c3b1535c4444f7b8a078c577078a705/bain_report-in_search_of_customers_who_love_their_bank-2018.pdf.

Bloomberg. "SBI YONO Has A Valuation Of Over $40 Billion, Chairman Rajnish Kumar Says." September, 2020. https://www.bloombergquint.com/business/sbi-yono-has-a-valuation-of-over-dollar40-billion-chairman-rajnish-kumar-says.

Businesswire. "Bank Customer Loyalty Declining: 47 Percent of U.S. Consumers Would Consider Target or Walmart as a Banking Alternative." April 19, 2016. https://www.businesswire.com/news/home/20160419005137/en/Bank-Customer-LoyaltyDeclining-47-Percent-of-U.S.-Consumers-Would-Consider-Target-or-Walmart-as-aBanking-Alternative.

Christensen, Clayton. Harvard Business Review. "The Essential Clayton Christensen Articles." January 24, 2020. https://hbr.org/2020/01/the-essential-clayton-christensen-articles.

Deloitte. "Deloitte Digital Banking Maturity Report." October, 2020. https:// www2.deloitte.com/content/dam/Deloitte/nl/Documents/financial-services/deloitte-nl-gx-fsi-digital-banking-maturity-2020.pdf.

Deloitte Insights. "Designing the modern digital function." January, 2021. https://www2.deloitte.com/us/en/insights/focus/industry-4-0/chief-digital-officer-digitaltransformation-journey.html.

Forrester Consulting. "The future of digital banking in Japan." October, 2021.

IBM Institute of Business Value. "Unlock the Business Value of Hybrid Cloud." 2021. https://www.ibm.com/downloads/cas/PG8BJ8EK.

McKinsey & Company. "AI-bank of the future: Can banks meet the AI challenge?" September 19, 2020. https://www.mckinsey.com/industries/financial-services/ourinsights/ai-bank-of-the-future-can-banks-meet-the-ai-challenge.

———. "A two-speed IT architecture for the digital enterprise." December, 2014. https://www.mckinsey.com/business-functions/mckinsey-digital/our-insights/a-two-speed-it-architecture-for-the-digital-enterprise.

———. "Welcome to the Digital Factory: The answer to how to scale your digital transformation." May 14, 2020. https://www.mckinsey.com/business-functions/ mckinsey-digital/our-insights/welcome-to-the-digital-factory-the-answer-to-how-toscale-your-digital-transformation.

———. "Why Do Most Transformations Fail?" July, 2019. https:// www.mckinsey. com/~/media/McKinsey/Business%20Functions/Transformation/Our%20Insights/Why%20do%20most%20transformations%20fail%20A%20 conversation%20with%20Harry%20Robinson/Why-do-most-transformations-faila-conversation-with-Harry-Robinson.pdf.

MIT SLOAN Management Review. "The New Elements of Digital Transformation." November, 2020. https://sloanreview.mit.edu/article/the-new-elements-of-digital-transformation/.

PwC. "Financial Institutions, Both Retail and Commercial, Have More Data on Their Customers Than Anyone Else." PwC. 2020.

Sironi, Paolo. "Banks and Fintech on Platform Economies: Contextual and Conscious Banking." Wiley. 2021.

Stoxx. "STOXX Changes Composition of Sector Indices effective June 22nd, 2020." June 13, 2020. https://www.stoxx.com/document/News/2020/ June/ Index%20Update_STOXX_Component_Changes_Sector_ Indices_20200613.pdf.

The MIT Initiative on the digital economy. "The Platform Era Unfolds." August, 2019. https://ide.mit.edu/insights/the-platform-era-unfolds/.

Printed in Great Britain
by Amazon

21080327R00160